From Yao to Mao: 5000 Years of Chinese History
Part III

Professor Kenneth J. Hammond

THE TEACHING COMPANY ®

PUBLISHED BY:

THE TEACHING COMPANY
4840 Westfields Boulevard, Suite 500
Chantilly, Virginia 20151-2299
1-800-TEACH-12
Fax—703-378-3819
www.teach12.com

ISBN 1-56585-869-7

Kenneth J. Hammond, Ph.D.

Associate Professor of History, New Mexico State University

Ken Hammond was born and raised in Ohio and received his B.A. from Kent State University in History and Political Science. In the early 1980s, he studied and worked in Beijing, China, then entered Harvard University for graduate study in 1987. He received his A.M. in East Asian Regional Studies in 1989 and a Ph.D. in History and East Asian Languages in 1994.

Dr. Hammond joined the faculty of New Mexico State University in 1994 and has taught there since that time. In 2000, he became department head in history. He teaches courses in Chinese, Japanese, and Korean history and in East Asian gender history. He has also been active in developing Asian Studies at New Mexico State and in establishing exchange programs between NMSU and schools in China and Korea.

Dr. Hammond's research focuses on the cultural and intellectual history of China in the late imperial era, from the 10th through the 18th centuries, especially the history of the Ming dynasty, from 1368 to 1644. He has published articles and translations on Chinese gardens, as well as essays on the 16th-century scholar-official Wang Shizhen. Dr. Hammond also edited *The Human Tradition in Premodern China*, a biographical reader for undergraduate students.

In 1999, he received an American Council of Learned Societies research grant to spend five months at the Chinese Academy of Social Sciences in Beijing. In 2002–2003, he was an Affiliated Fellow at the International Institute for Asian Studies at Leiden, the Netherlands. In June 2003, he organized and chaired an international conference on Chinese cultural history in Leiden.

Dr. Hammond is past president of the Society for Ming Studies and has served on the Board of Directors of the Southwest Association for Asian Studies.

Table of Contents

From Yao to Mao: 5000 Years of Chinese History
Part III

From Yao to Mao: 5000 Years of Chinese History

Scope:

The 36 lectures in this course explore the history and culture of China, spanning a vast temporal and spatial domain and developing several themes to help understand this ancient and complex society. We will proceed in an essentially chronological passage through the unfolding of China's political and cultural evolution, with particular attention to important ideas and individuals and the roles they have played in shaping both China's historical past and its dynamic present.

Chinese civilization originated in the confluence of several regional Neolithic cultures nearly 5,000 years ago. Emerging from the mythological Era of Sage Emperors, such as Yao and Shun, China's historical record begins with the Shang dynasty around 1500 B.C.E. We will follow the growth of China from a small kingdom on the North China Plain to a major empire extending from the Siberian frontier to the jungles of Southeast Asia, from the Pacific coast to the Central Asian deserts.

One of our main themes will be the evolution of social and political elites and the mechanisms by which they acquired and asserted their power as rulers of China. Closely linked to this is the history of political thought in China, from shamanistic roots in prehistory through the Axial Age of Confucius and Laozi and the long process of crafting and adapting the Imperial Order over the past two millennia and more.

We will also be concerned with the ways in which the Chinese have thought and written about themselves and the world around them. Cosmological ideas about the nature of the universe, the metaphysical insights of Buddhism and religious Daoism, and the perennial mysticism of popular religion have blended and interacted throughout Chinese history in ways which have yielded both the beauties of art and the horrors of religious conflict.

Throughout these lectures, we will consider China's history as it relates to the world beyond China. For more than 2,000 years, China has been linked to the global economy, and traders and travelers have brought both the riches of the empire and tales of its splendor to the West. We will trace the increasingly close relations between

China and the West from the age of the Mongol conquests in the 13th century through the rise of European imperialism in the 19th and into the present age of China's reemergence as a great world economic and political power.

By engaging with the history of China over the last five millennia, we will become familiar with one of the world's greatest civilizations and, arguably, its most persistent. Far from the popular image of China as a stagnant, unchanging relic of a once glorious past, we will see China as a living culture that has flourished and declined, revived and returned to greatness several times over thousands of years. We will come to understand some of the key features that allowed China's political order to remain stable for more than 2,000 years and that continue to shape this country at the opening of the 21st century.

Lecture Twenty-Five
The Rise of the Manchus

Scope:

The late 16th century once again saw a small group of people on China's northern frontier begin to build their power and prepare to challenge China militarily. Nurhaci was a Jurchen, a descendant of the people who had ruled north China in the 12th and early 13th centuries. He built a multi-ethnic alliance he named the *Manchus* and led them to dominance in the area that is today called Manchuria. Under his son and grandsons, the Manchus launched a campaign to overthrow the Ming and conquer China. As China faced internal rebellion in the early 1640s, the Manchus seized the moment and were able to gain control of Beijing in June 1644. After further campaigns in central and southern China, their Qing dynasty consolidated its rule over China proper and went on to expand the empire in Inner Asia.

Outline

I. The Manchus were a creation of Nurhaci in the late 16th and early 17th centuries.

   A. Nurhaci was Jurchen who dreamed of reviving the Jin dynasty.
      1. Born in 1559, he conceived the ambition of uniting the peoples of the northeast and challenging China's dominance.
      2. He first gained leadership over the Jurchen in the late 16th century.
      3. He then created a new "super-ethnic" group by allying with neighboring groups.

   B. Nurhaci forged a shared identity for these people and shared his vision of expansion with them.
      1. In the first quarter of the 17th century, the name *Manchu* was invented, perhaps based on the Buddhist figure Manjusri.
      2. A written script for Manchu was created.
      3. A putative history of the Manchus was developed and began to be written down.

4. Links were established with other peoples on the northern frontier of China, especially the Mongols to the west.

II. From 1626, the Manchus began to challenge the Ming for power.

A. A revived Jin dynasty was proclaimed in 1626.
1. This was meant to signal the Manchus' imperial ambitions.
2. They established a capital city at Mukden, modern Shenyang, based on the design of Beijing.
3. In 1635, the Manchu language was made the official court language.

B. The Qing dynasty was established in 1636.
1. The new name recognized the fact that the Manchus were more than successors to the Jurchen.
2. *Qing* means pure and symbolized the Manchu ambition to cleanse China of what they claimed was the decadent corruption of Ming rule.

C. Military campaigns against the Ming began in the late 1630s.
1. The siege of Jinzhou in 1641 was a major victory for the Manchus.
2. Some defeated Ming generals brought their troops over to the Manchu side.
3. By early 1644, the Manchus controlled all the territory outside the Great Wall to China's northeast.

III. In 1644, the Ming faced twin crises that toppled the dynasty.

A. The internal woes that had plagued China since the Wanli era led to massive rebellions.
1. Fiscal problems and factional conflicts weakened the government and impeded its ability to deal with floods and bad harvests.
2. By the time a new emperor came to the throne in 1628 and began reforms, it was too little, too late.
3. Peasant rebellions broke out in the northwest and southwest.

B. By the early 1640s, the rebels threatened the survival of the dynasty.
1. The biggest force was led by Li Zicheng in Shanxi province west of the capital.

2. In the spring of 1644, Li led his forces in an attack on Beijing and, in April, was able to enter the city.
3. The last Ming emperor hanged himself, and remnants of the court fled south to Nanjing.
4. Li Zicheng proclaimed his own dynasty and set out to create a new government.

C. The Manchus took advantage of this chaos in China to effect their own conquest.
1. A Chinese general named Wu Sangui was guarding the pass in the Great Wall where the wall reaches the ocean.
2. He was worried about the situation in Beijing, perhaps because his mistress was there and he thought she might be forced to become a concubine of Li Zicheng.
3. Wu allowed the Manchus through the Wall to aid in chasing the rebels out of Beijing.
4. After Li's army was destroyed, the Manchus refused to depart and, instead, announced that their Qing dynasty would now rule China.

IV. The Qing conquered all of China over the next 20 years.
A. Most of the fighting took place between 1644 and 1646.
1. The greatest resistance came in the Jiangnan region.
2. The siege of Yangzhou and the massacre of its citizens after their surrender was a message to all not to resist too long.
3. The Ming court fled south, and the last Ming prince was eventually captured and executed in 1660.

B. Some resistance continued until the 1680s.
1. Ming loyalists withdrew to Taiwan and created a fortified retreat there.
2. Coastal raiders and pirates allied with the Ming exiles.
3. Finally, in 1683, the last of the challengers to Qing power was suppressed.
4. The new dynasty entered on a great age of expansion and prosperity, which we will examine in the next lecture.

Essential Reading:

Pamela Kyle Crossley, *A Translucent Mirror*.

Supplemental Reading:

Frederick Wakeman, *The Great Enterprise*.

Questions to Consider:

1. Why did Nurhaci feel the need to include other ethnic groups in his quest for a new power to challenge China? Why did he not simply seek to revive the Jurchen and restore the Jin dynasty?

2. Why would Chinese commanders have gone over to the Manchu side rather than remain loyal to the Ming dynasty?

Lecture Twenty-Five—Transcript
The Rise of the Manchus

We've been talking about the crises, the gridlock that had afflicted the Ming dynasty from the end of the 16th through the first few decades of the 17th century. Many of the factors that we've looked at in this were internal, were domestic: concerns about the political factionalism that was centered on the court and the imperial bureaucracy; problems in the economy; problems with the emmiseration of peasants in parts of the country where tax burdens had been made heavier by the conversion to cash. But while all that was going on within the Ming system, outside of China—off in what is now in northeastern China, but which was then beyond the frontier—a new force was developing that would come to be the successors to the Ming, would come to overthrow the last remnants of the Ming dynasty and conquer China in the middle of the 17th century, and that force was in the form of a new people.

It's not often that we get to talk about the idea of a new people, people that we call the Manchus. Prior to the late 16th century, there were no Manchus; there was no one called by that name, no one with that sort of identity. The Manchus were, in a sense, a created ethnicity, a created culture, and they were the creation of a man named Nurhaci. Nurhaci was himself a Jurchen—and remember we talked about the Jurchen as one of the non-Chinese people who had invaded the north of China, conquered it back in the early 12th century and established the Jin dynasty, which controlled north China until the Mongol conquest early in the 13th century. Nurhaci was a Jurchen. The Jurchen people, after the fall of their dynasty, had returned to their traditional life in the forests and valleys of what is now northeastern China.

Nurhaci was born around 1559, and as a young man he conceived the ambition of restoring the glory of his people, regaining the power and prestige which they had possessed when they had invaded and conquered north China and established the Jin. But he soon began to feel that the Jurchen people by themselves would not perhaps be the best vehicle for these ambitions. He created a super-ethnic group by getting other tribal groups, tribal communities in the vicinity of the Jurchen people, to affiliate with his movement. In some instances, he did this via conquest; in some instances he did this via what we might think of as diplomacy, by negotiating agreements and arrangements with other peoples in the area. In the first quarter of the 17th century, this newly forged group began to call itself, and began to be referred to, as the Manchus. We don't know exactly where the term Manchu itself comes from. It may be derived from the name of a Buddhist spiritual figure called Manjusri, who is a spirit of wisdom and very popular particularly with Mongolian Buddhists; and Mongols and the Manchus communicated with each other a lot, shared a lot of ideas.

Wherever the name came from, this is how they began to identify themselves, and the Manchus adopted a writing system. They began to write down their own legends, their own myths. They created a history of the Manchu people, with an origin myth and a long account that included the history of the Jurchen, but expanded to have a more comprehensive kind of perspective. They developed their relationship with the Mongols who lived, not in the mountains and valleys of the northeast, but out on the grasslands further west, through a number of links. Some of these had to do with religion— the adoption of Buddhism by many Manchus was part of this process—and the writing system, which the Manchus used as they began to record their legends and histories, was based upon the rating system of the Mongols. So, they made a variety of cultural connections and cultural links.

Through most of this period, through the first quarter of the 17th century, the Manchus seemed to have principally been concerned with developing their own sense of identity, their own internal organization, their own consolidating their position in the territories which they already occupied; but as we moved into the second quarter of the 17th century, the Manchus began to directly challenge that the Chinese, the Ming dynasty, for power, first in the northeast and then later as we'll see in China itself. The Great Wall of China forms the cultural frontier along most of its length. Inside the wall, and to the south of the wall, is the area of settled agricultural society that we associate with Chinese civilization. Beyond the wall, to the north or west of the wall, are the areas of semi-nomadic peoples with civilizations, with cultures that are very different from those of China.

In the Ming dynasty, the Great Wall really was the frontier for most of its length; but at the very eastern extremity of the wall, where it comes down to the sea, Chinese settlers had moved outside the Great

Wall and had settled and what is now southern Manchuria. When the Manchus began to conceive and act on the ambition of challenging the dynasty, this was the first area of activity. In 1626, they signaled their ambitions by proclaiming a revived Jin dynasty, what they called the "later Jin" dynasty. This was a signal that they intended to try and reclaim the heritage, reclaim some of the glory of their ancestors. They established a capital city at what is now the site of the city of Shenyang. The Manchus called it Mukden, and it was built along the same layout, with the same design as the Chinese capital at Beijing. So this again was a signal, a representation of their imperial ambitions. Also in 1635, the Manchu language, which was largely based upon Jurchen language, was made the official language of the court.

The next year, in 1636, the name of the dynasty was changed. It was changed from Jin, which means gold—which was also the surname of many of the Manchus, including the most powerful family—and the new name was adopted. The new name that was adopted was the Qing dynasty. Qing is a Chinese term, it means pure. The symbolism here was that, on the one hand, there was an ambition to do more than simply revive the heritage of the Jin. They wanted to go beyond what the Jurchen had achieved earlier—not simply a partial conquest of China, but a complete takeover. The other aspect of the symbolism of the title Qing was to purify China, to purge the empire of the corrupt elements, which they attributed to the decadence of the Ming dynasty. Of course, this kind of symbolism, this kind of rationale for the overthrow of a dynasty, is itself embedded in Chinese political traditions. It's an echo; it's a reflection of the doctrine of the Mandate of Heaven, which of course, as we've discussed earlier, goes all the way back to the very origins of Chinese political history.

In the 1630s, particularly towards the end of the 1630s, beginning of the 1640s, military campaigning against the Ming became more active and moved up to larger scale operations. In 1641, there was a great siege at the Ming garrison at a place called Jinzhou, outside the Great Wall; and eventually the Manchus succeeded in capturing the fortress, and this was a great victory for them. It became an even greater victory in that several of the generals of the Ming army who had been defeated, then defected, went over to the Manchu side; they apparently felt that the Manchus did have the Mandate of Heaven, that their power was on the rise, and they chose to associate themselves with that new reality. By early 1644, the Manchus had established their control over all of the northeast, right down to the line of the Great Wall. They had not been able to penetrate the Great Wall, but they had now controlled the territory beyond the wall, all the way up into their ancestral homeland.

The situation in 1644 in China was pretty bleak. As we've talked about before, the crises that had been building up at the end of the 16th and the beginning of the 17th centuries had not been addressed by the Ming states. The imperial government was ineffective; it was locked up by internal factional conflicts, by the moralization of political debate and discourse, which meant that compromise and pragmatic policy solutions were much more difficult to produce and to put into effect. The financial problems of the dynasty had begun to intensify as well. In the northwest and the southwest, the areas where commercialization had not advanced as far, the rationalizations, the reforms of the tax system that had been put in place back in the 1570s finally began to really have some very negative effects. Larger and larger numbers of farmers were not able to maintain their tax payments. The process of selling their crops, getting their copper coins, converting those to silver, and then paying their taxes in silver was not a very good one for them, and it led to increasing defaults, loss of property and a growing landless group within the peasant population.

Even in the areas of the country where commercialization was well developed, problems began to occur as we moved into the 1620s or 1630s, because the flow of silver into the country began to decrease. The silver coming out of Japan dried up almost completely because the Japanese had put export controls on silver. They didn't want silver leaving their economy. The silver coming into China from the new world, from the Spanish mines in Latin America, also began to decrease. It didn't stop by any means; it continued to flow in. But the rate at which new silver was coming into the Chinese economy began to fall, and that meant—along with the Japanese situation—that as the economy was growing and expanding, that money became scarcer, and this of course led to various kinds of problems.

The factional conflicts at the court in the 1620s were very brutal and very bloody, but they are brought to an end finally in 1628, when a new emperor comes to the throne and when the power of the last of the great "evil eunuchs," as they're called, was broken. The political infighting really comes to a close for the most part. It doesn't disappear entirely, but it ceases to be such a powerful block on the effectiveness of government action. After 1628, the new emperor embarks on a process of reform trying to get the dynasty back on line. The problem is that it's really just too little too late. He does some good things, he makes some sincere efforts, but the problems that have begun to beset the empire are simply beyond his capacity to resolve with the kinds of resources that he has at his disposal.

Through the 1630s, the situation, particularly in the northwest in what is now Shanxi province, just gets worse and worse. Large numbers of farming families are dispossessed, are wandering on the roads; and not surprisingly, as we've seen in earlier instances, they begin to organize themselves and be organized into rebel bands. Larger and larger bodies of armed men with no vested interest in the stability of the present order begin to raid, to attack small towns and administrative centers, to try to simply seize the livelihood that they need, to break into government granaries to get food, to raid government treasuries to get money, and this pattern of rebellion needs to be addressed by the government by deploying troops. The problem is that the lack of revenue, the decline in tax revenues, means that sometimes the troops don't get paid, unpaid troops will sometimes defect to the other side, and the situation then of course simply continues to deteriorate.

By the end of the 1630s, and as we move into the beginning of the 1640s, one individual emerges as the main leader of these rebel movements in northwest China, and this is a man named Li Zicheng. Li Zicheng didn't have any particular political program. Unlike the founding of the Ming dynasty, when Zhu Yuanzhang positions himself at the head of a great mystical peasant movement, it doesn't appear that there was a particularly well-developed spiritual or religious program in the 1630s. It was more simply a struggle for survival, a struggle by these groups to overthrow the existing authority and perhaps establish conditions or circumstances in which their particular livelihood would be better guaranteed. Li Zicheng leads a large peasant army to the north in the course of the early 1640s. There's a lot of fighting in northern Shanxi, and this is not far from the imperial capital at Beijing.

Finally, in the spring of 1644, Li Zicheng is positioned to make an attack on the capital itself. He leads his forces towards the capital from the northwest, and finally, in April of 1644, is able to enter the capital and seize it and occupy it for himself. At this time, this is the final tragic moment for the imperial court. The story is that on the morning when the rebels had seized the city, the last of the Ming emperors gets up in the palace and goes into his audience hall, only to find that all of his officials have fled. The court had departed overnight, but somehow no one had felt quite ready to tell the emperor this. The emperor realizes that the situation is hopeless. He walks—which was unusual for emperors—out of the palace to the north, and goes up a hill, what's called Coal Hill, which is an artificial hill, built up out of the dirt that had been dredged from the moat surrounding the palace. He took with him a bit of silk, and when he reached near the top of the hill, he cut himself, cut his finger and wrote on this piece of silk the two characters, which mean the son of Heaven, the official title or name for the emperor, the most convenient way to refer to the emperor. He then tied a sash around his neck and hanged himself from a tree on this hillside, and that brought the rule of the Ming dynasty effectively to an end.

Li Zicheng was in control of the city. The officials of the court and some princes of the imperial family were fleeing to the south; they made their way to Nanjing, which was the secondary capital of the dynasty, and they did hold out there for a while. There are efforts to proclaim a successor, but as we'll see, none of those will really work out. In Beijing, Li Zicheng proclaims a new dynasty of his own, with himself as the new emperor, and he begins to undertake the process of trying to establish himself in the palace. He puts up notices calling on officials of the former dynasty who are still in the capital to present themselves at his court, promises that they'll be pardoned, they won't be punished if they show up. A few actually do, and he begins the process of trying to put a new governmental regime together. But this doesn't last long because the Manchus have not gone away, and nor have all the loyalists of the Ming dynasty itself.

Over at the eastern end of the Great Wall, at a place called Shanhaiguan, which means the pass between the mountains and the sea. Its the place where the wall comes down out of the mountains and runs right down to the coast, there's a great fortress, and it is at that fortress that the Manchus had been stopped in their efforts to come into China previously. The commander of that fortress is a man named Wu Sangui. Wu Sangui was a general in the Ming army and was a very good general—that's why he had been given responsibility for such an important position—and he had exercised that command quite effectively, keeping the Manchus on the outside of the wall and his Chinese forces on the inside.

However, when Li Zicheng captures Beijing, Wu Sangui finds himself in a difficult situation. He is still a Chinese general and is charged with protecting the empire from the barbarians, the Manchus, the outsiders, but now his dynasty's in trouble. His emperor is dead, and perhaps a more direct concern to him, his mistress is in Beijing, and he is worried that she may perhaps be recruited into the harem of the new emperor, Li Zicheng, if he succeeds in establishing himself in power. Wu Sangui makes a very difficult choice. He negotiates with the leaders of the Manchus. He works out an agreement with them, under the terms of which he will allow the Manchus to bring their army inside the Great Wall in through the Shanhaiguan pass. The Manchus and Wu Sangui's forces will then go to Beijing and overthrow Li Zicheng, drive the rebels out of the capital and restore the Ming dynasty.

The Manchus agree to this. Wu Sangui opens the gates and together they go west to Beijing, where they do indeed drive Li Zicheng out of the capital and destroy his nascent effort at establishing a new dynasty. Having done this however, and not surprisingly, the Manchus announced that they are not, in fact, going to restore the Ming dynasty and then withdraw and return outside the Great Wall, but that they are putting their Qing dynasty in place in Beijing and seizing the capital for themselves. Wu Sangui, having achieved perhaps his real objective, which was getting Li Zicheng out of the capital and making sure that his particular interests were secure—and of course, being something of a realist—accepts the reality of the Manchu conquest, and in fact, becomes a general in the Manchu military. Having seized the capital was a very important step of course, but there was a lot more to the Ming dynasty, a lot more to the empire than the capital itself. The Manchus then had to set about establishing their rule over the rest of the empire, and this was not an easy or simple process.

Most of the military campaigning that was involved in the conquest of China takes place over the next two years, between 1644 and 1646. As in previous conquests, particularly if we look back at the example of the Mongol conquest in the 13th century, the greatest resistance to the Manchus came from the Jiangnan area, an area near the mouth of the Yangzi River, where the Yangzi comes out to the sea, which was the wealthiest area, the area where the greatest concentration of literati could be found, where the developed commercial economy in conjunction with these very ancient traditions of Chinese culture and elite life meant that—perhaps a sense of, I suppose we could say patriotism—at least, a cultural resistance to barbarian invasion was greatest. It was in the Jiangnan area that we see the most dramatic efforts to fight off the Manchu conquests. This has come to be symbolized, perhaps most powerfully for the Chinese, by the story of Yangzhou.

Yangzhou is a city actually on the north side of the Yangzi River along the Grand Canal, a great commercial city, and a city famous for its painters, for its poets, for its luxurious lifestyle. The Manchus arrived to besiege the city is 1645. It put up a fierce resistance, much more than the Manchus had expected, and when finally the city was surrendered, the Manchus took a very savage vengeance upon it. For ten days, there was basically the looting and killing of anyone that was found, any Chinese that were found in the city. The massacre of Yangzhou became a symbol. On the one hand, a symbol of for the Manchus, a message that they were sending to the Chinese saying that if you resist, if you hold out too long and miss the opportunities to surrender which we will extend to you, this is the fate which you can expect to suffer; on the other hand, it becomes a symbol to the Chinese of the barbarism of the conquerors and of the heroism of the Chinese who had resisted and had chosen death to rather than surrender. This becomes a motif, which returns in later Chinese history, particularly at the end of the Qing dynasty. The legacy of Yangzhou is often invoked at the end of the dynasty as an appeal to Chinese patriotism and nationalism in the early 20th century.

The Ming court, which had fled from Beijing, even though the emperor had not managed to escape with it, settles into Nanjing. The Manchus arrive and besiege Nanjing; the court eventually flees from there. A series of princes are named as emperors; none of them remains as emperor very long, they're captured they're killed one after another. The end of the 1640s has brought most effective resistance to the Manchus to an end. A remnant of the court flees to the far southwest, and the last claimant to the imperial throne, the last direct legitimate successor to the title of emperor for the Ming, actually flees the country and goes into what is now Burma and remains there as an exile until 1660, by which time the Manchus are firmly in control of the southwest, and they negotiate an agreement with the Burmese rulers, under the terms of which the last of the Ming royal families are returned to China, turned over to the Manchus, given a very nice banquets, and then executed.

That brings the dynasty to pretty much an absolute end, although there are still some loyalist elements that hold out, particularly on the island of Taiwan. Taiwan at this time is in a very peculiar circumstance because it is part of China. It's technically part of Fujian province on the southeast coast, but it has become a focal point for activity by Westerners. In particular, the Portuguese and the Dutch have a presence on Taiwan; and in addition to these foreigners, there are what are called pirate groups, sea raiders that are based on Taiwan. Ming loyalists cross the straits and go to Taiwan and hold out there as well without ever making much of a serious attempt to return to the mainland; but nonetheless, their presence is an irritant to the Manchus. It's not until 1683, that the last remnants of Ming loyalism over in Taiwan are finally suppressed. So, it takes almost 40 years from the beginning of the conquest in 1644, with the Manchus' entry through Shanhaiguan, until the very last vestiges of Ming loyalist resistance are put to rest.

But by the 1680s, the new dynasty is on a very firm footing. A new emperor is on the throne, and the Qing is about to settle into a prolonged period of peace and prosperity, not unlike the long age of the middle Ming. After the turmoil of the founding and the usurpation of Zhu Di, the Ming dynasty, as we've seen, settled into a fairly long period of stability, prosperity and growth; and we see perhaps an even greater example of this in the story of the Qing dynasty from the late 17th through the 18th century. We'll take that story up in the next lecture.

Lecture Twenty-Six
Kangxi to Qianlong

Scope:

From 1661 to 1795, China was ruled by just three emperors; Kangxi, Yongzheng, and Qianlong. Kangxi and Qianlong each occupied the throne for 60 years, giving this period almost unparalleled stability. It was largely an age of peace and prosperity for China, though warfare continued on Inner Asian frontiers almost throughout these reigns. Chinese people, whether members of the educated elite or simple farmers, had to adjust to life under the Manchus, who imposed some of their own particular cultural practices on their new subjects. The requirement to wear the *queue*, the long braid characteristic of Manchu warriors, was imposed on pain of death as a sign of China's submission. Yet during the long *Pax Sinica* of the late 17th and 18th centuries, a Manchu-Chinese symbiosis developed that provided a strong and durable basis for the dynasty and allowed Chinese scholars and officials to make major political and cultural advances.

Outline

I. The Kangxi emperor oversaw the stabilization of the dynasty and its early expansion.

    A. Kangxi came to the throne as a young boy in 1662.

        1. He was not the eldest son of the previous emperor but had survived a bout with smallpox and was seen as the strongest.

        2. His uncle Oboi and a council of regents guided his early years, but in 1667, he took power into his own hands.

        3. He reigned until his death in 1722.

    B. In the 1670s, he faced the only serious challenge to Qing power until the middle of the 19th century.

        1. Wu Sangui, who had aided the Manchus in their initial conquest and been rewarded with a large grant of territory in southern China, led a rebellion against the Qing.

        2. Other Chinese generals in the south joined him.

    3. It took the Qing eight years to suppress the rising, but the main Chinese armies remained loyal to the dynasty, and the Qing emerged stronger in the end.

C. Once peace was restored in China proper, Kangxi turned his attention to Inner Asia.

    1. The main objective was to bring all the Mongol tribes into the empire.

    2. Eastern Mongols had shared in Manchu power from the first.

    3. Western Mongol groups resisted incorporation, some fleeing as far as southern Russia.

    4. Kangxi's campaigns did not resolve this problem but did extend Qing power into what is now Xinjiang (New Frontier) province.

D. Kangxi also established a new fiscal basis for the empire.

    1. In 1712, he issued an edict fixing tax rates on land throughout the empire.

    2. This was based on a survey carried out to determine who actually owned and farmed specific plots of land.

    3. The edict decreed that these tax rates would remain in effect in perpetuity, laying the foundation for later fiscal problems.

II. Kangxi died in 1722 and was succeeded by one of his sons, who became the Yongzheng emperor.

A. Yongzheng came to the throne in questionable circumstances.

    1. The edict naming him emperor was believed by many to have been forged.

    2. He was the 13th son of Kangxi, far from first in the normal line of succession.

    3. He imprisoned or exiled several of his brothers.

B. Yongzheng set out to reform the finances of the dynasty.

    1. Already the adverse effects of the 1712 taxation edict were being felt.

    2. Yongzheng attempted to increase the flow of taxes to the central treasury, while regularizing the financing of local administration.

    3. This move was resisted by an alliance of local elites and officials, who wanted to retain control of revenues and informal income, sometimes seen as corruption, in their own hands.

    4. Eventually, Yongzheng had to abandon his reforms.

C. He did, however, succeed in streamlining some aspects of government.

    1. He simplified the central policy-making bodies and began the process of creating the Grand Council, which became the main organ in the imperial government.

    2. He also carried out important reforms in domestic policy, such as ending discrimination against certain groups of "inferior" status.

III. Yongzheng reigned for 13 years and was succeeded in 1735 by the Qianlong emperor, one of the greatest rulers in Chinese history.

A. Qianlong continued the long age of peace and prosperity in the empire.

    1. He managed the government and the economy in a pragmatic way, relying on the advice of his Confucian officials but always paying close attention to the day-to-day workings of government.

    2. China's population approached 400 million by the end of the 18th century.

    3. China was the richest country in the world, and Chinese products flowed around the planet in the ever-expanding global economy.

B. Qianlong completed the process of bringing the Mongol tribes into the empire.

    1. In a series of military campaigns through the 1760s and 1770s, he subdued vast territories in Central Asia.

    2. He pursued a policy of honoring defeated leaders with titles and riches and, thus, won the loyalty of many.

    3. He extended Qing authority into Tibet and pushed the empire's borders to their greatest extent.

C. But by the end of his reign, new problems began to develop.

    1. Given existing technologies and patterns of land tenure, the growth of China's population began to push against ecological limits.

    2. Standards of living stagnated in the later 18th century.

3. China began to feel new pressures brought on by changes in the outside world.
4. The rise of an aggressive, expansive system of state-sponsored capitalism in the West began to lead to a conflict between the Atlantic world and East Asia, the background to which we will discuss in the next lecture.

Essential Reading:

Jonathan Spence, *K'ang-hsi, Emperor of China.*

Supplemental Reading:

Susan Naquin and Evelyn S. Rawski, eds., *Chinese Society in the Eighteenth Century.*

Philip A. Kuhn, *Soulstealers: The Chinese Sorcery Scare of 1768.*

Questions to Consider:

1. Given the harshness of the conquest, how were the Manchus able to win the support of the Chinese in the middle decades of the 17th century?
2. The tax edict of 1712 effectively prevented later emperors from adjusting the fiscal system of the dynasty. Why would Kangxi have thought this was a good or reasonable thing to do?

Lecture Twenty-Six—Transcript
Kangxi to Qianlong

The Manchu people conquered China in the middle of the 17th century. They came across the Great Wall with the connivance of the Chinese general Wu Sangui in 1644, and after seizing the capital and fighting campaigns over the next couple of years in central China, they basically were in control of the empire. Certainly, by the time the last claimant to the Ming throne was executed in 1660, the dynasty was essentially secure.

In 1661, the first emperor of the Qing dynasty, called the Shunzhi emperor, died and was succeeded by one of his sons, who began a series of only three emperors who preside over the empire for the next 135 years. The reigns of the Kangxi, Yongzheng and Qianlong emperors cover the central part of the Qing dynasty, and in some ways these three emperors represent the greatest achievements of not just the Qing dynasty, but Chinese civilization in general. The peace and prosperity and stability over which they presided was also a great age of culture, and art, and literature, and many of the other things that we identify with the greatness of Chinese civilization.

The Kangxi emperor, when he comes to the throne in 1662, in the first year of his reign, comes to the throne as a boy. He was only about eight years old when he succeeded, but he was chosen for some very particular reasons. He was not the oldest son of the Shunzhi emperor, but he had already survived the disease of smallpox. This was taken as a sign of his heartiness, of his fitness, and so he was chosen and accordingly made emperor, and at first was guided in his rule by a council of regents, members of the Manchu imperial family headed by his uncle, a man named Oboi, what's called the Oboi regency is the first 5-6 years of Kangxi's reign. At the end of that time, in 1667, when he was still just a mid-teen, he decided to take power into his own hands and contrived to have is uncle Oboi set aside and have the regency disbanded; and from that point on rules in his own right. He comes to power in his own right. He begins to exercise his authority directly at a time when apparently things were stabilizing and the dynasty was going to settle into its normal course.

But in the 1670s, he does face what is the most serious challenge to the power of the Qing dynasty, certainly since its establishment, and what will be the last serious challenge to it until the middle of the

19th century. What happens is that Wu Sangui, who we've talked about earlier—Wu Sangui was the Chinese general in command of the fortress along the Great Wall that was keeping the Manchus out, and it was his decision to try to ally with the Manchus to drive the peasant rebels led by Li Zicheng it out of Beijing in the summer of 1644 that allowed the Manchus to come in and get the conquest really underway—had been rewarded for his cooperation with the Manchus by being given a very large territory in southwestern China, essentially as his own feudal domain, and a couple of other important Chinese generals who had cooperated with the Manchus had been similarly rewarded.

They had held these now for some 30 years, but in the 1670s, perhaps in anticipation of generational change, would these territories be handed on to their heirs, the Manchus tried to recover direct control of this part of southwest China, and this triggered a rebellion, and Wu Sangui becomes the leader of this rebellion. It's sometimes called the Rebellion of the Three Feudatories, because Wu and the other two generals rose up to defy the power of the dynasty. Other Chinese military forces in south and southwest China joined in with this rebellion, but not all of them, and not Chinese armies elsewhere. It took the Qing dynasty some eight years to put down the Rebellion of the Three Feudatories. It isn't finally completely suppressed until the early 1680s. But the success that the dynasty had in controlling it, containing it and eventually putting it down was based on the loyalty, which the vast majority of the Chinese army displayed towards the new dynasty.

This was a very significant development because it showed that the Manchus, the Qing state was not perceived as an alien body. It wasn't seen as something which needed to be resisted and done away with. Despite the fierceness with which the conquest had been resisted at the time, by the 1670s, the Manchus had managed to establish sufficient legitimacy, a sufficient sense of loyalty amongst the Chinese that when Wu Sangui led this great rebellion, the vast majority of the Chinese military remains loyal to the dynasty. The Manchus had achieved this largely because after the initial conquest they had established conditions of peace within the empire and had allowed, for the most part, the Chinese to return to their normal livelihoods. They had not sought to transform China; they had not sought to excessively punish China. Certainly they had imposed taxation and had imposed particularly heavy taxation on the Jiangan and they had also established the requirement that Chinese men adopt the Manchu hairstyle, what's called the queue.

The queue is a long braid worn down the back, with the front half of the head shaved. This was the traditional Manchu hairstyle, and now Chinese men were required to adopt it under penalty that if you didn't wear this particular hairstyle, you could be executed, so it was a very severe measure, but once a generation or so had passed, it was so widely accepted that it became part of almost the sense of Chinese identity, and the community of interest between the Chinese population, the Chinese armies and the Manchu dynasty. The Qing dynasty was such that the loyalty of the troops remains in place, and Rebellion of the Three Feudatories was indeed suppressed. Once this challenge to the power of the Qing had been overcome, Kangxi was free to turn his attention to other concerns.

Perhaps most important on this list was trying to win control over all of the Mongol tribes. The Mongol peoples were scattered over a wide geographic areas. Some Mongol groups, the eastern Mongols, were quite close geographically to the homeland of the Manchus, and they had been closely allied with the Manchus and participated in the conquest of China, participated in the government of China. Manchus and Mongols had almost a partnership in rule over the Chinese. The Manchus were clearly the dominant group, but the Mongols played a very significant role as well, and these were primarily the eastern Mongols. Western Mongol groups, groups of Mongol tribes located further away from the Manchu homeland, had not joined in, had not come to share the same interests as the Manchus, and indeed some had moved quite far way to remove themselves, to be away from the turmoil in China and the ambitions of the Manchus. Some had gone as far as southern Russia.

Kangxi begins to pursue a number of efforts to try to win these Mongol tribes back, to try and incorporate them into the Qing Empire. The Qing Empire becomes, in a sense, a kind of multi-ethnic state. You have the Manchus as a conquering elite; you have, of course, the vast body of the Chinese people, but you also have other non-Chinese groups that are incorporated within the empire, the Mongols most significantly, Tibetans as well, as we'll see, and this effort to bring central Asian peoples, not just the western Mongols but Turkic peoples as well into the fold was pursued by Kangxi and by his successors.

He does not resolve this. Kangxi is not successful ultimately in either militarily defeating the western Mongols or in diplomatically luring them back into participation in the Qing political order; but he does start this process in motion, and it will be carried on by his successors as well. He also is able to project Qing power into new geographic areas, not necessarily as far as will ultimately be the case, but he begins to create direct Qing administration in the far west, in what is today still called Xinjiang, which is a Chinese term that means new frontier, and the far west of China becomes the new frontier of the Qing empire beginning under the reign of Kangxi.

These extra concerns, these frontier or borderland concerns, are one aspect of Kangxi's rule. Another is his effort to stabilize the fiscal basis for the dynasty. He undertakes in 1712, a great survey of the empire, and now we know that this process of surveying the empire, of trying to ascertain who owns land and what kind of land it is and what the taxes should be, this is a very important function of the imperial state. It is often done in conjunction with the founding of a dynasty; it sometimes is done later in the course of a dynasty to try and reform the fiscal system. We saw Zhang Juzheng's attempt to do this back in the 1570s. Now in 1712, the Kangxi emperor carries out this kind of a survey and fixes tax rates based upon it. But he adds a new wrinkle, which is that he proclaims that the taxes based upon this survey of 1712, will remain in effect in perpetuity. They will always remain as they have been fixed under the survey of 1712, and this comes to be known as the Tax Edict of 1712. It lays the foundation for some serious problems in the financing of the dynasty in later times.

In 1722, the Kangxi emperor died after being on the throne for 60 years, and he is succeeded by one of his sons, who becomes the Yongzheng emperor. When Yongzheng comes to the throne, the circumstances of his succession are a little unusual. Indeed, some Chinese historians, some Chinese at the time, questioned the legitimacy of his succession. He was the 13th son of the Kangxi emperor, so he was far from the head of the queue, head of the line to become emperor; and yet, he is named in an edict, which was purportedly written by the Kangxi emperor on his deathbed. Some, if not most Chinese, however, believed this edict to have been forged. The conduct of the Yongzheng emperor after coming to power also tended to generate a certain amount of suspicion as well because he had very bad relations with most of his other brothers, and he had almost all of them—there are only 1-2 with whom he seemed to get along very well—he had almost all his other brothers either imprisoned, exiled, or in some instances murdered. However he came to the throne, the perception was that it was not necessarily the most proper of successions.

Nonetheless, the Yongzheng emperor turns out to be pretty good emperor. He doesn't have a long reign, but he devotes himself during the years that he's on the throne to trying to improve the administration of the empire, to make it more efficient and more effective, and in some ways more compassionate, more benevolent. His biggest challenge, not surprisingly, has to do with the financial system. Already in the 1720s, the effects of the 1712 tax edict are beginning to be felt. The flow of income to the imperial treasury was not what Yongzheng thought it should be. There were problems in the collection of taxes out in local communities. There were problems in the transmission of taxes to the capital. Taxes would basically be collected on a local level, forwarded up to a provincial level, consolidated there and then shipped off to the court, to the capital in Beijing. Financing for local administration was then, in theory at least, to be returned from the imperial treasury to the provincial, and from the provincial to the local levels.

These various stages of transfer were fraught with the potential for corruption and problems of various kinds. One particular issue, given that taxes were being paid in silver, was that some people's taxes were paid in relatively small quantities of silver. These were often melted down to be consolidated into bars of silver, which could be transported more simply, and there were a number of fees and charges and surcharges that were added on to cover the meltage fees and the loss that might occur in consolidating these, so that there were various irregular duties, irregular taxes that were being imposed by local officials. These taxes tended not to become part of the official records, tended not to make their way to the capital, and so Yongzheng was concerned about abuses of the system and about trying to improve the flow of income to the center and to make sure that the court had the greatest degree of control over the tax system.

He tried to reform the system in ways which would eliminate some of the informal charges that were being imposed at the local level. He did this by sending out officials from the court and sending out instructions from the court to local administrators. He experimented with this in a couple of provinces in central China first to ensure that money that was collected was properly recorded, money that was submitted to the imperial treasury was properly handled, and he allowed the officials to retain a portion of revenues directly in the localities so that they could finance local administration without having to have money go all the way to the capital and then make its way it all the way back.

In the test provinces in central China where these policies were explored, they worked very well and he was very pleased with them in the 1720s. But when he tried to apply them on an empire-wide basis, he ran into a lot of resistance. The reason for this was basically that the provinces where he had experimented with these reforms in central China were neither the richest nor the poorest part of China, a cross-section or middle range of the economic and social life. When he attempted to apply these policies in the wealthier areas, particularly along the coast, he ran into a lot of resistance, again from local elites and from local officials who really wanted to have informal control over revenue flow rather than more direct control from the central government.

This is reminiscent of themes that we've seen earlier on: the resistance to Zhang Juzheng's reforms; the resistance to Wang Anshi's reforms back in the Northern Song dynasty. It's a classic pattern of conflict of interest within Chinese fiscal administration and within Chinese political culture in general. The Yangzhong emperor eventually becomes frustrated with his efforts to reform the financial system, and he abandons, in the early 1730s, his efforts to impose this new regime and acquiesces in the informal charges that are being imposed in local contexts. So, it's a frustrating story for him. He's obviously a very well intentioned emperor, and he sets out to make these reforms, and he has some initial success, but is ultimately thwarted by the power of the local elites, the power of the literati in their capacity as both local officials and private economic interests.

Other aspects of administration were more effectively reformed under the Yongzheng emperor. In particular, he begins a process which comes to fuller development under his successor in the form of what comes to be called the Grand Council. In the Ming dynasty, we talked about the functioning of the Grand Secretariat after 1380, when the first Ming emperor Zhu Yuanzhang had abolished the position of chief minister and had assumed those functions for himself. Later in the Ming dynasty, the Grand Secretariat emerges as the principal center of political activity, of policy debate and policy formulation within the Ming government. The Grand Secretariat continues to exist in the Qing dynasty, but it comes to be supplanted in its central political function by what we call the Grand Council, which was perhaps an even more informal body than the Grand Secretariat itself.

As it begins under Yongzheng, and as it develops under his successor, the Grand Council is almost entirely a deliberative and consultative body. It doesn't have so much of the administrative paperwork functions that the Grand Secretariat did. Those indeed remain lodged in the Grand Secretariat, and the Grand Council becomes more purely a policy-debating forum. It doesn't have a fixed membership. Individuals are appointed to serve on the Grand Council; they serve at the pleasure of the emperor. Its size varies, sometimes as few as three, sometimes as many as 8-9 members, but it becomes the most critical decision-making entity within the Chinese administration. This is begun under Yongzheng. Yongzheng also was very concerned about the well-being of his subjects. He undertook some reforms to regularize or normalize the status of certain social groups who were considered to be outcasts or pariah groups. He made a number of these kinds of efforts to moderate the conditions of difficulty under which certain elements in Chinese society lived.

Yongzheng, as I say, was not on the throne for a real long time; he reigns for 13 years. When he dies in 1735, he's succeeded by one of his sons, who becomes the Qianlong emperor. Qianlong reigns from 1735 until 1795. He actually lives until 1799; he abdicates in 1795 in order that he will not serve on the throne longer than his grandfather, Kangxi. Kangxi reigned for 60 years; Qianlong reigns for 60 years. Many Chinese and Western historians view the reign of Qianlong as the high tide of the Qing dynasty. The 60 years were a period where the achievements of the early Qing, many of them come to fuller fruit; and Qianlong completes a number of the tasks, a number of the projects that his predecessors had gotten underway. He managed the government. He oversaw the economy in very pragmatic ways. He was a very hands-on administrator. He paid close attention to the details of many aspects of what was going on in the empire. He oversaw military affairs. He was very concerned with the tax system, he was eager to appoint and give power to competent officials, but he always made sure that he knew what they were doing, not necessarily to micromanage them, but simply to simply keep himself as well informed as possible about the workings of government administration.

Under the Qianlong emperor, the population continues to grow in China, reaching perhaps 400 million by the end of the 18th century, and China attained perhaps its greatest prosperity, certainly prior to the present day. It was probably the richest country in the world, a country whose products—tea, silk, lacquer ware, ceramics, other kinds of manufactured goods—flowed all around the planet in a global market in which China came increasingly to form a very powerful component. Some 25 percent of global economic production originated in China, and many of the goods that were produced there traveled by land or by sea to the far corners of the earth. So the empire over which Qianlong presided was truly one of peace and prosperity, certainly in terms of China itself.

Nonetheless, it was not a time when there was peace everywhere, and for Qianlong in particular; there were military campaigns that he was very interested in pursuing. He was able to complete, through these military campaigns and through diplomatic initiatives as well, the process of bringing all the Mongol tribes into the empire. The western Mongols—sometimes called the Junghars—finally, by the 1770s or so, submit to the authority of the Qing. They return to Chinese territory or to Qing territory in the far west, and they pay their respects, they pay their feudal duties to the Qianlong emperor, and he receives them in a special ceremonial sites built specifically to perform these functions. Qianlong pursues a policy, a very careful policy in dealing with defeated rivals, of paying them great honor and great respect. He gave them official titles; he often bestowed great wealth upon them. He was interested in expanding his empire; he was interested in establishing his control and domination. He was not interested in destroying and humiliating his enemies. He wanted to bring them into the empire and then once he had them in the empire, he wanted them to be successful, prosperous participants in this great all-encompassing vision that the Manchus had.

He deepened the relationship between the Qing Empire and Tibet. Tibet had been closely linked to the Mongols, and through that link to the Mongols was incorporated into the Manchu empire when it was first established in the 17th century. The Manchus had been deeply involved in the internal politics within Tibet. The conflicts between different factions within the religious leadership in Tibet was resolved under pressure from, and perhaps with the assistance of the Manchus, and the Qianlong emperor continues those policies of intervention and maintaining a strong Qing presence in Tibet all through his reign. Under the Qianlong emperor, the borders of the empire reach their greatest extent. Everything that is today part of China and much more what is today the Republic of Mongolia and the maritime provinces of Russia, and certain territories in central Asia that are now not part of China, were part of the empire under Qianlong. He really takes the empire to its greatest extent.

By the end of his reign, by the middle of the 1790s, new problems, new challenges begin to emerge, many of which are the result of the long period of success that the dynasty enjoyed. The growth of China's population had begun to push up against the ecological limits of Chinese territory. The amount of land which was available to sustain the population couldn't be expanded, and the intensity of its exploitation had limits that were based upon the very surplus of labor that was available for farming. Standards of living tended to stagnate in the latter part of the 18th century, the economy which had grown so much, seems to have simply plateaued, seems to have reached a point beyond which, given the existing technologies and patterns of land tenure and relations of production, it couldn't continue to grow.

At this same time, new pressures began to be placed on China from the outside world. In particular, the rise of a very aggressive and expansive system of state-sponsored capitalism in the West began to lead towards a conflict between the Atlantic-centered world and East Asia. We'll look at the background to that and bring the story up to the threshold of European-Chinese interaction in the next lecture.

Lecture Twenty-Seven
The Coming of the West

Scope:

Contact between Europe and China goes back to at least the time of the Roman Empire. For much of history, though, such contact was quite tenuous and infrequent. Marco Polo's visit in the 13th century and the reports of missionaries did little to engender clear knowledge about China in the West. In the 16th century, as Europeans began to explore and participate more fully in the global economy, information began to improve, but contacts remained marginal for both sides. With the Industrial Revolution and the rise of free-trade ideas in the West, a new age opened. For centuries, the economic relationship between Europe and China was based on Europeans buying Chinese goods with silver, much of it originating in the mines of Spanish America. By the end of the 18th century, the British, in particular, were eager to open broader trading relations and were desperate to find a commodity other than silver that they could trade for China's superior goods.

Outline

I. East Asia and the Mediterranean world had a long history of trade and contact.

   A. Overland and maritime links go back at least to the time of Rome.

   1. Roman glass has been found in Chinese tombs.
   2. Chinese silk was traded in markets in Rome.
   3. Chinese records contain reports of representatives of Rum arriving in Chang'an, but these were likely traders rather than true Roman diplomats.

   B. During the age of Islamic expansion, direct links were cut off, but trade continued.

   1. Christian Europe was isolated by the growth of the realm of Islam.
   2. Goods from East Asia, especially China, were still traded along the Silk Road and through maritime networks stretching from the Pacific through the Indian Ocean.

3. Arab traders from the Persian Gulf began to arrive in China in increasing numbers in the 7th century and established a mosque in Guangzhou around 670.

4. The Great Mosque in Xian also dates from the 7th century and was used by Muslims in the caravan trade.

C. In the age of the Mongol conquests, as we have seen, Europeans again traveled directly to China.

1. Representatives of the church sought to contact Christian communities in Inner Asia and founded some congregations in China.

2. Such traders as the Polos helped move goods and brought some knowledge of East Asia into Europe.

3. There were even brief hopes for a Christian-Mongol alliance against Islam at the time of the Crusades, based on myths of Prester John's Christian kingdom.

II. By the 15th century, Europeans had some knowledge of East Asia but would need to embark on the Age of Exploration to learn more.

A. The Portuguese began to search for a direct route to the source of valuable spices in what is now Indonesia.

1. They explored the coast of Africa and reached the Indian Ocean, finally arriving in India in 1496.

2. By 1511, the Portuguese had attacked and seized Malacca, one of the key ports in Southeast Asia.

3. The Portuguese found that they could not dominate the local trade system and, instead, sought to create a place for themselves to participate in this rich economic life.

4. The Spanish followed suit, as did the Dutch and the English after 1600.

B. Through the 17th and early 18th centuries, Europeans established a place for themselves but remained merely one group out of many participants in the Asian trade networks.

1. Rivalries between the Europeans further weakened their positions in Asia.

2. The Dutch came to concentrate on the islands of Southeast Asia and Japan, while the Spanish took over the northern Philippines.

3. The Portuguese diverted much of their attention to Africa and the New World, and the British came to focus on India.

4. For all the Europeans, though, China remained a great potential market and source of the highest quality goods.

III. Two major changes in the later 18th century set the stage for the complete transformation of the global economy.

    A. The Industrial Revolution took place, primarily in Britain.

        1. Although many of the conditions leading to the Industrial Revolution were also present in China and India, in England, the proximity of coal and the availability of new markets and sources for raw materials in America combined to set off a great leap forward.

        2. The English also appropriated technologies from Asian manufacturers that, when combined with new energy sources from coal and steam, yielded significant improvements in production.

    B. At the same time, Adam Smith's ideas about free trade became the ideology of British capitalism.

        1. In his 1776 book *The Wealth of Nations*, Smith argued that governments should refrain from intervention in the economy as much as possible and allow markets to function freely.

        2. This new way of thinking led to the abandonment of the old mercantilist system, which included state-sponsored trading companies, such as the English and Dutch East India companies.

    C. The combination of an expanding industrial economy, in need of raw materials and markets for its goods, with an assertive free-trade ideology created the conditions for the emergence of Western imperialism, led by the British in the 19th century.

        1. What was needed was some way to break in to the Chinese domestic market.

        2. In India, the British found their ideal commodity; we will discuss the creation of a new trading order based on opium in the next lecture.

Essential Reading:

Susan Whitfield, *Life along the Silk Road*.

Supplemental Reading:

Janet L. Abu-Lughod, *Before European Hegemony.*

Questions to Consider:

1. Although products, such as silk and glass, traveled long distances across Eurasia or the Indian Ocean, very few individuals made the journey from Europe to Asia or from Asia to Europe before the 16th century. Why was it easier for goods to be transported than for people to travel?

2. China remained a vast continental empire, but Europe was divided into small local states that constantly warred with one another. How might this situation have played a role in the development of relations between the two regions?

Lecture Twenty-Seven—Transcript
The Coming of the West

At the end of the 18th century, both China and the West were poised on the edge of a new era in world history. In China, the Qing empire, which had been around for more than 150 years, had achieved great success and expanded its territory, its population had grown, its economy had flourished, its culture was vibrant and dynamic; and yet, it carried within itself the seeds of very serious problems having to do with the pressures of population on the ability of the land and the economy to sustain it, and having to do with the ability of governmental machinery to deal with new changing circumstances and challenges that might arise.

In the West, the end of the 18th, beginning of the 19th century is a period where trends and developments that had been taking place—again both in the economic realm and the cultural and political life—were about to usher in a new age of expansion, of projection of power both in terms of trade and commerce, and in terms of military and political domination. What I want to do in this lecture is to step back from the immediate narrative that we've been following and look over a long view of the relationship between Europe and East Asia—China in particular—and how that developed, how it evolved, and what the particular circumstances are that bring us up to this great threshold at the end of the 18th century.

East Asia and the Mediterranean world—which might be a good way to think about Europe to begin with—have had a long history of trade and contact. We know that overland exchanges and maritime trade goes back at least to the time of the Roman Empire in the West, and probably long before that as well. But certainly by the time of Rome, we see Western products showing up in China and Chinese products showing up in the Mediterranean realm. Roman glassware in particular has been found in tombs dating from the Han period in China. Chinese silk was traded in the markets of Rome and has been found in the graves of the wives of Roman senators. Chinese records, the written historical documents of the Han and other early times, mention representatives from a place called Rum arriving at Chang'an, the great imperial capital. These may not have been representatives of the Roman government, but were more likely traders and perhaps were even intermediaries who were simply bringing Roman products, Roman commodities to China; but nonetheless, it indicates that the Chinese were aware of the existence of the Mediterranean world, were aware of other great states, other great empires located far away, but nonetheless with whom they were in these long-term exchange relations.

During the age of Islamic expansion, when we get down to the 7th century, the linkages that had been established between the West and East Asia were certainly disrupted. Christian Europe was isolated, was cut off from much of the rest of the Eurasian landmass by the movement of Islamic armies out of the Arabian Peninsula into the Middle East, into Persia across North Africa. This results, not in a complete rupture of trade, but certainly in breaks in other kinds of communication links. Commodities, goods, material things continued to travel, but knowledge, information, seems not to have been carried along to quite the extent perhaps that it had been earlier. Goods from East Asia, particularly China, were still traded overland, along what we call the Silk Road through central Asia and down through Persia and into the eastern Mediterranean, and maritime networks stretching from the Pacific, through Southeast Asia across the Indian Ocean, continued certainly to function quite dynamically.

Arab traders from the Persian Gulf, from the Red Sea, began to go from the Middle East across the Indian Ocean around Southeast Asia and began arriving in increasing numbers on the south China coast in the 7th century, bringing with them their new religion, the teachings of Islam. Indeed, a mosque is founded in Guangzhou, the great southern trading port sometimes known as Canton around 670, not long after the great age of Islamic expansion had begun. In Chang'an, now known as Xian, a great mosque also was established, this to serve communities of Arab traders coming overland across the central Asian routes, also late in the 7th century. These outposts of Islam, these termini for the maritime overland trading routes, remind us that while trade continued, it was perhaps in somewhat different hands. The Arab traders now came to control and participate in the commercial exchanges both overland and on sea, bringing goods of various types from China, from Southeast Asia, all the way to the frontier with Christendom at the end of the Mediterranean, at the eastern end of the Mediterranean. From there, these goods tended to cross over into the hands of the Venetians, who dominated the commercial trade of the eastern Mediterranean in terms of bringing goods from the markets of Damascus or Alexandria or Aleppo into the Western European economy.

As we've noted earlier, during the age of the Mongol conquests, when Mongol armies spread out from central Asia and extended their power over Persia and over other parts of Middle East into Russia, China, central Asia—all under the control of the Mongol people—this created conditions which allowed travelers, merchants, to cross the Eurasian landmass in greater security than had previously been possible, particularly during the age of disruption and the tensions and frictions between Islam and Christianity in the West. Representatives of the church, particularly the Catholic church, made their way across the trade routes and brought back accounts of China, and traders like the Polo family that we've talked about earlier—Marco Polo and his father and uncle—made journeys across from the Mediterranean to China to East Asia, not in great numbers, but at least in sufficient numbers so that their economic impact was noticeable and that some individuals like Marco Polo left written records of these journeys and these cultural encounters. So, the Mongol age was one in which communication resumed to a somewhat greater degree while the flow of goods continued.

There were even brief hopes during the Mongol period for some sort of Christian-Mongol alliance against Islam. The myths about Prestor John, the supposed Christian ruler of the kingdom in central Asia, fueled a lot of interest in Western Europe in what was going on with the Mongols, and what was going on at the other end of their empire. These didn't prove to be particularly substantive. The alliance between Mongols and Christians against the Muslims never really materialized, and history went on its way in the Middle East without this connection really amounting to much. Nonetheless, the information that began to arrive in the West about China, particularly through narratives such as that of Marco Polo, sparked new interest in the wealth and power that was out there far away as a lure to adventurers and profit seekers around the Mediterranean and in Western Europe.

By the 15th century, although the age of Mongol domination had passed away, Westerners had a better sense of what was going on in East Asia, but they wanted to find ways to learn more and to get better access. The Portuguese in particular come to play a very significant role in this process. The Portuguese are positioned at the far west of Europe. They're outside the Mediterranean, facing out on the Atlantic. They were not a position to be particularly competitive with the Venetians. The Venetians controlled much of the trade in spices that came in from Southeast Asia across the Indian Ocean, up through the Persian Gulf and the Red Sea and then into the Mediterranean zone, where the Venetians profited greatly from this. But for a variety of reasons, the Portuguese decided that they would like to perhaps make an end run around the dominance of the Venetians in this trade and seek a more direct access to the sources of wealth in the Far East without dealing with middlemen.

The problem, of course, was that they had to deal with Africa. Africa. They didn't really know how big it was, they didn't know how to get around it, they didn't know if it was possible to get around it, and so they began in the 15th century a very systematic process of exploration. Going down the African coast, charting the coastline, charting the waters as they went, and then returning to Portugal to report on what they had learned, to add more information to a growing database, and then to launch new expeditions that would go a bit further and gain a bit more knowledge and bring that back. There was a lot of excitement in the mid-century when they finally made their way around the great western extension of Africa and thought they could head east, but of course they then ran into the southern extension of Africa, and that led to further decades of exploration.

Finally, in the 1490s, they make around the southern cape of Africa and into the Indian Ocean, and by the mid-90s managed to get to the west coast of India. That results in the Portuguese having now direct access to the trading systems of Asia, of the Indian Ocean, Southeast Asia and beyond. What they found, however, was that they could not simply arrive on the scene and take over. They weren't strong enough; they weren't powerful enough to assert dominance over the system trading system. In 1511, they attacked and seized the port of Malacca, which is down on the Malay Peninsula, one of the key trading centers in Southeast Asia. They hoped that this perhaps would put them into a dominant position, but again they found even control of this very crucial entrepôt was not sufficient to give them the kind of control that they hoped for. They seem to have thought, in perhaps a somewhat arrogant way, that simply arriving on the scene would be sufficient for them to assert the superiority of themselves, of the West, of Christian civilization over the Asians, but that proved not to be the case.

Instead, what they realized eventually, certainly as we move on into the 16th century, was that there was tremendous wealth to be made not by taking over and dominating the spice trade from Southeast Asia all the way back to Europe, but by participating in the local trading networks of the Indian Ocean, of Southeast Asia and of East Asia, what comes to be called the country trade. Within these local trading networks, they began to carry cargoes, to establish a presence in courts all over the region and to do most of their economic activity within the local context, going back to Europe only occasionally and even then making most of their money not from the transportation of goods over these very long distances, but from the shorter trading excursions that they made within Asia and the Spanish followed suit. Beginning around 1600, the Dutch and the English also established trading companies to manage their affairs in Asia and became part of this same process, not of establishing dominance, but of becoming participants in a trading network, a trading system which was so extensive and so lucrative and so wealthy that there was enough for all of them to find profitable roles within it.

Through the 17th and into the 18th centuries, Europeans established a place for themselves within the existing Asian trading networks, but they remained merely one group out of many participants in this larger system. Rivalries between the European powers further weakened their positions in Asia. The Spanish and the Portuguese, the English and the Dutch, the northern Europeans versus the southern Europeans, Protestants versus the Catholics, a variety of divisions and rivalries served to undermine whenever coherence they might have had. There was not a single European presence, but rather each of them acted on their own, and often in conflict with one another. So that perhaps further prevented them from achieving any kind of true domination. The Dutch eventually came to focus their economic activity on the islands of Southeast Asia, what is today the country of Indonesia, and in Japan. The Dutch were able indeed, when Japan sought to close itself off, to restrict trade with outsiders, trade with foreigners, the Dutch managed to be the only foreigners, the only Westerners who were allowed to trade regularly. Twice a year they could send ships to Nagasaki, but all other Western traders were banned from Japan.

The Spanish, of course, established their position in the Philippines, and after 1571, when they took over Manila, which became a very lucrative center of trade for them. We've talked already about the role of Manila as the western terminus of what are called the Manila galleons, the great ships that sailed from Acapulco in Mexico across the Pacific, bringing silver from the Spanish mines in Mexico and Latin America, and Chinese traders who came from the southeast China coast over to Manila absorbed much of the silver and transported it back to China to pay for all the commodities, all the various goods that were sold to the Spanish. The Spanish would then transport these things back across the Pacific to Mexico; some of them stayed there, some of them eventually made their way across the Atlantic back to Europe.

The Portuguese, who had been the first to seek out a presence in Southeast Asia, maintained some role there. They had trading positions on the west coast of India, and of course in the 1530s established a small enclave at Macao, on the south coast of China, which remained in Portuguese hands until 1999, but they devoted much of their attention to Africa and to Brazil, and so did not become as significant a factor in the European presence in East Asia as they might have been. While the Dutch and the Spanish and the Portuguese were interested in their various localities, the British of course became very much involved in India. All the Western powers continued to see China as the greatest prize of all, but one which was very difficult for them to gain access to. They saw it as a tremendous potential market, a place where they could sell goods to a vast number of potential consumers; and of course, more realistically perhaps, they saw it as the source of high quality manufactured goods. These were what were in great demand back in Europe and in other places—the ceramics, the tea, the lacquer ware, other kinds of silks and textiles that were higher in quality and better in price than what was available in Europe.

At the end of the 18th century, as we get back to our threshold, we've talked about the situation in China and some of the problems that were beginning to emerge there towards the end of the reign of the Qianlong emperor; but in Europe at this time, in the West at this time, things were also moving through a period of great change, and there's really two principal areas that I want to look at with regard to this. The first should be familiar to most of us already, the industrial revolution. The industrial revolution, which takes place, certainly first and foremost in Britain, creates new conditions for the production of goods. The conditions that led to the industrial revolution, the technological circumstances, the economic factors, the nature of commodity production, the kind of market economy that the industrial revolution grows out of, many of these factors were also present in China, certainly in the Jiangan area, the very wealthiest and most commercialized part of China, and to a certain extent also in parts of India, particularly in the Bengal region of India, where rather similar economic developments had been taking place.

Nonetheless, it is in England that we see the industrial revolution actually taking place. There's a lot of debate about this, a lot of discussion about how this came to pass. Certainly, part of it was the proximity that British early industrial manufacturers had to sources of energy, in particular, coal. The existence of easily accessible coal reserves in close geographic proximity to centers of industrial activity meant that factories could grow and function more economically than in places where coal supplies and textile productions, for example, were separated by a long distances, which was certainly the case in China. The English were also very good at appropriating technologies, at seeing how an existing technology, functioning on the basis of human labor power could be adapted to the use of steam power, of energy produced using coal. In particular, they were able to adapt the textile weaving technology that they found in Bengal as they began to establish a greater presence in India; and by combining some of these large-scale loom technologies from India with steam power produced in England, were able to dramatically transform textile production and launch really this cutting edge industry of the industrial revolution.

The material aspect of the industrial revolution is one dimensional—the expansion of the capacity to produce goods, the reduction in the costs of production and mechanization and large-scale manufacture yielded changes in the technology, not just of producing goods, but of distributing them, changes in transportation technology; the building of railroads in the 19th century, different kinds of power, technological innovations in shipbuilding and in the powering of ships leading to faster transport in maritime communication; other kinds of technological innovations associated with the industrial revolution, some of which really didn't get put in place until later on in the 19th century. This material dimension of the industrial revolution creates a whole new platform for the production of wealth and the dissemination of those products into a global market. It changes the role that Europe had had within the larger global system from one of essentially consuming manufactured goods produced elsewhere to producing cheap manufactured goods, which they then meted to market elsewhere.

In conjunction with this material dimension though, and certainly playing a very powerful role in this overall process, is the rise of a new ideology in the West, and this is the ideas that we associate perhaps most classically with the work of Adam Smith. It was in 1776 that he published his book, *The Wealth of Nations*, and in that, Smith argues that government should basically refrain from intervention in the economy as much as possible and allow markets to function freely. This was quite a transformation, quite a change. The dominant mode of economic activity, certainly in terms of large-scale international activities, had been what's called mercantilism. Mercantilism was essentially state-sponsored capitalism. If we look particularly at the question of the relationship between Europe and Asia, we can see a couple of classic mercantilist enterprises in the Dutch and English East India companies.

These were royally chartered companies formed within just a couple of years of each other, around 1600-1603, and they had managed a trade between either Holland or England and the Far East. The English East India Company had come to concentrate its activities more and more in India, while the Dutch East India Company had concentrated its activities more and more in the islands of Southeast Asia, but they were very comfortable in terms of their organization and their animating principle. For Adam Smith, this was not the way to go. This was not the most effective way to promote trade and commerce. Of course, writing in 1776, the industrial revolution was barely getting underway, he was not really talking about the kind of industrial capitalist enterprise which becomes characteristic of the 19th century; and yet, the ideas of free trade, which Smith enunciates, really become most effective when they are placed in conjunction with the growth in the material capacity for production that the industrial revolution brings about.

At the beginning of the 19th century, what we find in the West, and most particularly in England, is a very potent combination of a developing industrial economy capable of producing goods in large quantities at relatively low prices, needing access both to raw materials and to markets for those manufactured goods, and possessing, in conjunction with that capacity, an ideology of free trade, which argues that markets everywhere should be open to everyone, and that the British as international traders should be able to go where they wish and deal with whomever they wish on terms basically of equality and open access. It's a very powerful ideology that challenges the existing dominance of the great trading companies and suggests that if the state is involved at all, it should be involved solely to the degree of creating those conditions which allow private economic interests to maximize themselves.

The British were trading with China already, but they wanted to trade more. They wanted to trade more with everyone. At the end of the 18th century, and as they moved into the beginning of the 19th century, they were looking for a way to break in to the Chinese market. They had been buying things from China for a long time; this was the basic economic relationship between China and the West for centuries, that they had things, the Westerners came and bought them, and they bought them using silver. Silver flowed into China steadily over the centuries, from the 16th century down to the end of the 18th century, beginning of the 19th century. The British needed some way to change that, to break that established pattern, to overcome that existing relationship. At the beginning of the 19th century, they found a way to do so, and we'll see how that story unfolds in the next lecture.

Lecture Twenty-Eight
Threats from Within and Without

Scope: In the first half of the 19th century, China began to face new challenges, some arising from within its borders and some arriving from the outside world. Domestically, the long era of peace and prosperity that had lasted into the late 18th century gave way to one of increasing economic, demographic, and social problems. China's population growth began to put serious stress on the empire's ability to feed itself, and economic problems limited China's capacity for expansion of production. Popular rebellions began to break out as living conditions deteriorated. At the same time, the British began marketing opium in China on a rapidly growing scale, reversing the flow of silver into China and creating a drain of money just when China was in need of greater capital for investment. Efforts by the Qing to stop or regulate the opium trade led to war with Britain in 1839. The Treaty of Nanjing, which ended the war in 1842, not only created de facto legalization of the opium trade but also forced open coastal ports to foreign traders.

Outline

I. At the end of the reign of Qianlong and the beginning of the 19th century, China was at a turning point in its modern history.

   A. The very success of the Qing state had created conditions that now began to undermine the dynasty.

      1. Population growth, which had been rapid during the long years of peace and prosperity, finally began to push against the available food supply, and little land was left to be brought into cultivation.

      2. Patterns of intensive labor utilization in agriculture had rendered technological improvements unprofitable.

      3. The wealthy elites of literati and merchants sought to protect their economic interests against state taxation and against the demands of the peasantry.

      4. Frustration and resentment began to be manifested in popular rebellions against landlords and local officials.

B. The international context was also shifting.

   1. From the middle of the 18th century, China had regulated its trade with the West through the Canton trade, also called the *cohong* system.

   2. Trade was permitted only at the port of Canton, or Guangzhou, in the far south, and had to be conducted through state-licensed brokers, known as *hong* merchants.

   3. The flow of silver into China continued as Western merchants bought large volumes of tea, silk, ceramics, and many other kinds of valuable commodities.

   4. But the changes in the West, as outlined in the previous lecture, were putting pressure on this system.

   5. In 1792 and again in 1816, the British sent diplomatic missions to seek open trade relations, but in both cases, they were rejected by the Qing.

II. As the British consolidated their control of large parts of India, they came into possession of the opium growing regions and found an ideal commodity to change their trading relationship with China.

   A. Opium had been known in China for a long time.

   1. It was produced in small quantities in the far southwest and had been used as a medicine for centuries.

   2. Non-medicinal use was banned by the Yongzheng emperor in the 1730s.

   B. The British destroyed the indigenous cotton industry in Bengal and other parts of India to convert farms to opium production.

   1. They first began trading opium in Southeast Asia and found that it was popular among the Chinese coolie workers there.

   2. Imports into China began in the early 19th century but only took off after the end of the Napoleonic Wars allowed Britain to refocus its attention on Asia.

   3. From around 1816 to the mid-1830s, the volume of opium shipped into China grew every year.

   C. The impact of the opium trade was dramatic.

   1. Millions of Chinese became addicts.

2. The British demanded silver in payment for opium, and the flow of silver, which had been heavily in China's favor, was rapidly reversed.

3. By the 1830s, China was losing silver at such a high rate that it began to face serious shortages of capital and prices were subject to dramatic fluctuations.

III. The Qing state faced difficult problems in responding to these challenges.

   A. The government had become bureaucratically rigid.

   1. Efforts to deal with problems creatively were frustrated by established interests.

   2. Revenues were declining, which limited the capacity of the government to fund reforms or maintain infrastructure.

   B. Control of the opium trade was opposed by the British.

   1. The Qing repeatedly protested to the British about the evils of opium and its adverse impact on the Chinese economy.

   2. The court called for policy ideas from officials across the empire.

   3. Lin Zexu, an experienced official who had been serving in Central Asia, proposed a mix of rehabilitation for addicts and strict prohibition of imports and sales.

   4. Lin was named Imperial Commissioner to eradicate the opium trade.

   C. When China tried to stop the trade, Britain went to war.

   1. In 1839, Lin confiscated opium held by British merchants and arrested some leading British traders.

   2. The British argued that the real issue was free trade, and when the Chinese destroyed the opium, the British declared war.

   3. British military superiority inflicted serious defeats on the Chinese.

IV. The Opium War of 1839–1842 ushered in a new age in China's relations with the outside world.

   A. In 1842, the Qing were forced to sign the humiliating Treaty of Nanjing; although it never mentioned opium, the treaty had the effect of legalizing the trade.

1. The treaty required the Chinese to open ports along the coast to British and other foreign traders.
2. The treaty allowed British merchants to trade freely in China, without using the *cohong* brokers.
3. It ceded Hong Kong island to Britain.
4. It established the Principle of Extraterritoriality, which decreed that while British citizens were in China, they would be subject to the laws of Britain, not China.

B. In the wake of China's defeat, other Western powers also signed treaties.
   1. These expanded the rights of foreign powers in China.
   2. They included the "no most favored nation" clause, which ensured than any privilege granted to any one power must be granted to all.
   3. Foreign missionaries were given legal protection to operate in China.
   4. All these provisions opened China to the power of the West and led to severe disruptions of the domestic economy and political order.
   5. In the next lecture, we will turn to one of the stranger results of this situation, the Taiping Rebellion.

Essential Reading:

Frederick Wakeman, *Strangers at the Gate*.

Supplemental Reading:

James Polachek, *The Inner Opium War*.

Questions to Consider:

1. Opium was illegal in England, yet Parliament voted to go to war to force China to open its markets. How is this different from the "war on drugs" of the present period?

2. Why were the Chinese so reluctant to open their domestic markets to the outside world?

Lecture Twenty-Eight—Transcript
Threats from Within and Without

We come now to the great turning point in modern Chinese history—and in some ways in world history—that the beginning of the 19th century represents. From this point, until very recent times, the story of Chinese history that we've been following goes on to a rather negative decline, a rather negative trajectory. Problems arise that have been building up both within China and coming to China from outside, and it is at the beginning of the 19th century that we begin to see these manifest themselves in much more serious ways. The end of the reign of the Qianlong emperor in the mid-1790s is a good marker. It's a convenient historical line of delineation, demarcation where we can see that the very successes that the dynasty had achieved have begun to bear negative fruits.

Population growth, which was a sign of the prosperity and stability and peace of the Qing Empire, and which had been quite rapid, brought up to about 400 million people by the beginning of the 19th century, has started to push against available resources, the food supply. The land available for cultivation simply reaches a point that it can't yield much more, given the existing technologies and forms of cultivation and organization. The elites, whether they were the traditional elite of literati or the new elites of merchants, were very conservative, very concerned with protecting their wealth, their economic interests. We've seen, particularly for the literati, how repeatedly in the late imperial era of China, they had resisted efforts by the state to rationalize fiscal administration, to extract greater revenues from private sources. At the beginning of the 19th century, the strength of the literati elite remains very powerful, and with the passing of the Qianlong emperor, we get a succession of emperors. We move into a period where, although there are still good emperors, they're not as powerful, they're not as charismatic, they're not as dynamic as Kangxi and Qianlong in particular had been.

Frustrations, resentments among the populace begin to manifest themselves in the form of rebellions. It had been a long time, over a century, since there had been large-scale insurrections, of popular movements directed against the Qing, but beginning late in the 18th century, and then accelerating in the beginning of the 19th century, new forms of mystical movements amongst the peasantry, new forms of popular insurrection begin to break out, targeting both private interests—local landlords, local wealthy families—and the representatives of the state, the local officials. As we've noted, the international context was also shifting. Trade becomes the great question. We've talked in the last lecture about the industrial revolution, about the rise of the doctrines of free trade, particularly flowing from the thought of Adam Smith; and both the increased economic capacity of the West, and the changing ideology of free trade, begins to come into conflict with the established relationship between China and the West, and particularly China and England at this turning point of the 18th to 19th century.

From about the middle of the 18th century, China had regulated its trade with the Western countries to what's called the Canton system, the Canton trade or sometimes called the *cohong* system. Under this system, trade only could take place in one location, in one port, which was Canton—or Guangzhou in Chinese—in the far south, as far away from the imperial capital as could reasonably be done; and that trade had to be conducted through middlemen, through agents, Chinese agents who were licensed by the state and who served as brokers between Western businessmen and Chinese businessmen. These individuals were known as the *hong* merchants. This trade did function, it was quite a lively trade, but it was essentially a trade in which, as had been the pattern for centuries before this, the Western merchants brought silver to China, and with that silver they then bought Chinese commodities—tea, silk, ceramics, lacquer ware, other kinds of manufactured goods, which were in great demand in the West.

This regulated system, this controlled system of trade, was quite satisfactory to the Chinese; they were certainly making a lot of money, and they had good outlets for their manufactured goods. It was in some ways satisfactory to the Western merchants because they were certainly acquiring goods which could be sold profitably in the West, but there was a sense that there was still some great untapped potential, that there was still a tremendous amount of wealth to be had in dealing with China, if only a way could be found to sell the Chinese something which the Westerners had, which the Chinese wanted, and which the Chinese themselves would be willing to pay for, to pay perhaps not just in trade goods, but in silver, to reverse the flow of silver into China and start to balance it out a little better between the Europeans and the Chinese.

In 1792, and again in 1816, before and after the Napoleonic wars, the great age of disruption in European affairs, the British sent diplomatic missions to China to try to open trade relations, or to try to establish what the British thought of as normal diplomatic intercourse and commercial relations between England and the Qing government. In both instances, these missions were received very politely, but were told essentially that the Chinese were simply not interested. There's a very famous letter that the Qianlong emperor writes and sends to King George III in which he thanks the British King for his interest, but says, "We have everything that we need within our empire; we have no need for the shoddy goods that you can offer us. We welcome you to come and trade with us, but it has to be on our terms and in our way." This was considered unacceptable by the British, who were increasingly fueled by the passionate ideology of free trade and saw the Chinese as being not simply reluctant to enter into a proper trading relationship, but completely anachronistic; indeed, essentially began to see the Chinese as barbarians for their refusal to recognize the desirability and the legitimacy of an international trade regime based upon the ideas of Adam Smith.

The key to all this remained the question of what did the British have that the Chinese might want to buy? After about 1816, after the Napoleonic wars are over and the British are able to devote their attention to all this more seriously again, they finally come up with the key that unlocks the door to the wealth of China. That key proves to be opium. Opium was a substance that was already familiar to the Chinese. It was produced in relatively small quantities in the far southwest of China. It was known as a medicine, as a substance that could be used for certain particular utilitarian purposes for a very long time. Its non-utilitarian purposes, its non-medicinal purposes had also been known and recognized in China for a long time, and indeed one of the things that the Yongzheng emperor had done back in the 1730s as part of his social legislation was to impose regulations on opium, to restrict its use, to outlaw it as a recreational drug. The Chinese were aware of opium and aware of some of the problems that perhaps came along with it.

What the British found was that as they came into possession of increasing territories in India and particularly in northeast India around Bengal, that they found the environment there, the farming conditions there, particularly suitable for the cultivation of opium.

Opium was already grown there, but what the British did was to first go about undermining the existing cotton industry, in part of course because they didn't want competition with their expanding cotton industry and textile industry in England, but also because they wanted to convert the land which was being used for cotton production to opium production; and so, this was done very aggressively, very assertively by the British authorities, and this resulted then in having access to a large and growing supply of opium.

They then discovered, first in Southeast Asia and then much more extensively in China, that they could market opium, particularly to the poorest strata of society, although people on all levels of Chinese society came to consume opium; and they discover that indeed in south China, there was a tremendous amount of potential demand for this commodity. They began to ship opium in ever-increasing volume from Bengal, from eastern India, around through Southeast Asia and up to the port at Canton, where it was offloaded and entered into the domestic economy of China. Between 1816 and 1830, the volume of opium shipped from India to China increased significantly every year. The impact of this trade in China was dramatic. Millions of Chinese became addicted to opium. It became a tremendous social problem; people were not productive people. The same kinds of concerns with crime and antisocial behavior that we associate with certain drug problems in contemporary society begin to manifest themselves in southern China in the context of the growing opium trade.

On an economic level, the British were demanding payment for opium in silver. This had the effect quite rapidly of reversing the flow of silver. Silver had been flowing into China. China had run a positive trade balance in terms of silver with the Western countries for centuries. In the decades from the mid-1810's to the mid-1830s, that completely reverses, and silver begins to flow out of China at a very rapid rate, so much the than it leads to economic disruptions throughout the empire and starts to cause all sorts of adverse ripple effects within the domestic economy. This, of course, comes to the attention of the government quite profoundly. By the 1830s, there were shortages of capital for investment, prices were subject to dramatic fluctuation as the money supply was destabilized by the outflow of silver, and these kinds of economic effects, in addition to the adverse impact on social life that opium was having, began to be taken quite seriously by the Chinese government.

The Qing state, however, was having problems dealing with these kinds of challenges. The government had become increasingly unresponsive. Conflicts, policy debates within the Qing leadership had bogged down efforts to deal creatively with problems, were particularly frustrating because the bureaucratic mentality of always doing things the way they've always been done was quite strong; and so, to try to propose new solutions, to try to find ways to address problems that weren't based on well-established precedent, this was very difficult. Revenues were declining. The outflow of silver and its adverse effects upon the economy meant that taxes were not being collected as extensively, and the capacity of the government to maintain its normal functions, to simply do things like maintain the infrastructure of the Grand Canal, which tends to silt up and needs to be dredged and maintained in various ways, money for these kinds of activities began to become hard to come by, and this resulted in further problems; and of course, each of these problems as it develops only aggravates the existing ones, and the situation tends to go from bad to worse.

The Chinese realized that the opium trade was in many ways at the heart of their problems. It was a serious concern in terms of its social impact, and it was a serious concern in terms of its economic impact. The emperor began to seek ways in which to address this problem, seek ways to control the trade or indeed to eliminate it. Opium was after all illegal as a recreational drug in China. It was, of course, not widely available in that sense in the West either; the West was certainly aware of the adverse effects, the British were very aware of the adverse effects of opium. The Qing government repeatedly protested to the British authorities, to British traders and to the representatives of the British merchants about the evils of opium and its adverse effects on Chinese society and economic life. The emperor then called for a debate amongst his officials about how best to deal with this problem. Many expressed their opinions; there's a very lively policy discourse around this.

One individual in particular caught the emperor's attention, and this is a man named Lin Zexu. Lin Zexu was an experienced official. He had served in central Asia in dealing with the security problems that the Qing faced with the Muslim populations in central Asia, and he had distinguished himself as an official who was able to be flexible and creative in dealing with problems, and who was concerned not merely with the formalities of effective government, but with addressing the needs of the subjects, addressing the needs of the people. Lin Zexu submitted a proposal, a memorial to the emperor, in which he suggested basically a two-track approach to the opium problem.

On the one hand, he had a rather compassionate program towards individuals who had become addicted to opium. He advocated rehabilitation programs; in essence, job retraining programs, things that sound very familiar to modern-day social reformers to address the bad effects that opium addiction was having on people, to help them to shake their addictions, to give them ways to achieve more functional, more meaningful lives, and basically to address the demand for opium through these kinds of programs. At the same time, the other aspect of his program was one of strict prohibition of imports and sales. This was, after all, already the existing law; he simply advocated that it be enforced quite stringently. He felt that a combination of attacking the supply of opium by going after those who were importing and selling it, and undermining the demand for opium by providing these various social and rehabilitation programs for addicts, that these two approaches would in combination served to eliminate this problem.

The emperor was very impressed with Lin Zexu's memorial, and it was debated and discussed at court; eventually, in 1838, Lin Zexu was named to be imperial commission in charge of eradicating the opium trade in Canton. He travels south from the capital to Canton in the winter of 1838-1839, and in 1839, is finally ready to launch a serious campaign directed at stopping the flow of opium into China. He takes a very direct approach to this. In Canton, the foreign traders had warehouses—what they called factories, or sometimes they were called go-downs—places where their goods were brought ashore and stored before they were shipped off into various destinations in the interior. Lin Zexu, in the spring of 1839, ordered that the opium, which was held in these warehouses, be confiscated. A large quantity of opium was accordingly seized, and he had a large trench dug in the ground, and the opium was poured into this trench, dumped into the trench. Lime was then spread over it, and the whole concoction was burned. I gather that the lime was meant to, in some way makes the burning of it more effective and less dangerous.

When the Chinese destroyed these opium supplies, the British merchants, of course, were quite upset, and they demanded that something be done. The British military representatives at that time assured the merchants that they would be compensated by the crown, by the British crown, but Lin Zexu proved to be intent upon keeping the trade under control, keeping the trade shut down, and so the British, who thought that perhaps this was just a one-off demonstration, and that some more pragmatic solution, which would allow them to continue to trade, might be found, were quite upset when it turned out that Lin Zexu had no intention of allowing the trade to resume. After a second round of destroying opium, and no compensation being forthcoming, the British decided that they had to take action.

The British debated this. There was quite a debate in Parliament over what to do about China. It is a debate, which is framed largely, not in terms of the opium trade, but on the more lofty principles of free trade in general. The British do not wish to present themselves, of course, as a drug cartel—which is essentially what they were—but instead argued on the basis of an economic doctrine. When war is declared, and when the British fleet is sent out to attack China, it is done, not on the basis of making the world safe for drug dealers, but on the basis of promoting the doctrines of free trade.

British military superiority, which was unquestioned at that time—the British fleet, British armaments, the industrialized British military which had technologically been upgraded very significantly by the transformations of economic life in the West since the end of the 18th century—the British were able to inflict humiliating defeat upon the Chinese, and did so repeatedly. The war begins in 1839. It goes on until 1842. There are a series of periods of great activity. British naval forces sail into the various ports along the south China coast and shell the cities, terrorizing the local population. When they come far enough north and begin to look like they might approach the imperial capital region, the Chinese enter into negotiations, but those negotiations go on over a very long time. The British launch a second phase of military activities, which brings them very close to the capital in the north, and this finally impels the Chinese to reach a settlement.

That settlement takes the form, in 1842, of what's called the Treaty of Nanjing. Signed between the British and the Chinese government, the Qing government, it did a number of things. It opened a series of ports along the south China coast to British traders and allowed them to establish commercial residences in those ports—these come to be known as the treaty ports, of course based on the Treaty of Nanjing itself—and, they could trade freely without using the cohong brokers. It ceded the island of Hong Kong, which had been occupied by the British and used as a base; it ceded that to Britain for 100 years. Eventually, of course, that is expanded, and territory adjacent on the mainland is added to that, and that all remains in British hands until 1997.

The Treaty of Nanjing also established a very important principle, which is called the "Principle of Extraterritoriality." The Principle of Extraterritoriality basically says that while British citizens are in China, they will be subjected not to the laws of China, but to the laws of Britain. In other words, if they commit a crime in China, they will not be arrested and the prosecuted by the Chinese authorities, but will be dealt with by the British. This was in response to a number of instances in which British sailors who had been ashore in Canton had been involved in violent incidents of one type for another and had been arrested and prosecuted by the Chinese and were treated in ways which the British felt were inappropriate for subjects of the crown; and so, to protect foreigners in China, particularly the British, they imposed the element of extraterritoriality in the Treaty of Nanjing.

The Treaty of Nanjing is signed in 1842. In rapid succession over the ensuing 2-3 years, other Western powers also signed treaties with China. The United States signs its first treaty in 1844. The French, the Dutch, the Russians, all get in on the action fairly quickly. These treaties, each one adds a little more to the concessions which are being extracted from the Chinese. More ports are to be opened. A very important feature of these treaties is that they include what's called the "no most favored nation clause," which says that any concession which is granted to one power in a treaty automatically extends to all the powers which have treaties with China. This shares the benefits of imperialism amongst the foreign powers. Foreign missionaries were given legal protection to operate in China, to go into the interior on their proselytizing work.

These provisions, the various aspects of the Treaty of Nanjing, are quite humiliating for the Chinese. China had, of course, always thought of itself in some ways as the center of the known world. The very name that's used for China in many instances, Zhongguo, means the middle kingdom, the central kingdom. The traditional system of international relations in East Asia was one which was very focused on China as the center. When the Chinese dealt with the Westerners prior to the Opium War, they dealt with them as people who came almost from outside the realm of civilization. Now to be defeated militarily, to be forced to sign treaties which opened up Chinese territory to the residence of foreigners, which took away from a Chinese the ability to govern and regulate trade, this was a tremendous blow to the sensibilities of the Qing government and of the Chinese people in general.

The opening of the treaty ports beyond this psychological dimension had significant economic impacts. Of course, the extension of the opium trade further exacerbated the problems associated with that, but even where there were in some ways positive impacts economically, where trade expanded or where the ports grew in their own context, the dislocations that this caused in other parts of the Chinese economy sometimes were quite severe. This sometimes led to rather unanticipated consequences, and we'll explore one particular instance of that, that gives rise to a great rebellion, the Taiping Rebellion, in the next lecture.

Lecture Twenty-Nine
The Taiping Heavenly Kingdom

Scope:

The stresses within Chinese society that were growing in the early 19th century led some Chinese to search for radical new ways to deal with the world around them. Christian missionaries from the West began to make greater headway in seeking Chinese converts. In this context, one of the more intriguing episodes in Chinese history unfolded. This lecture will trace the course of the Taiping Rebellion, in which a tiny cult begun by Hong Xiuquan, who believed himself to be the younger brother of Jesus Christ, blossomed into a mass movement of tens of millions and nearly brought the Qing dynasty to an end. By the time imperial troops destroyed the last of the Taiping forces in the mid-1860s, some 20 million people had died as a result of war and related disasters. The dynasty survived but never fully recovered from this trauma.

Outline

I. The combination of internal and external problems gave rise in the mid-19th century to a profound challenge to the Qing dynasty.

    A. In southern China, the negative impact of the opium trade and the results of the ensuing war caused widespread suffering.

        1. By the 1840s, large numbers of people saw their lives disrupted by changing trade patterns and by the corrosive social effects of opium.

        2. The Hakka people, a linguistic and cultural minority, were particularly affected.

        3. Even members of the educated strata felt the tensions in social and economic life.

    B. Hong Xiuquan was a failed examination candidate who founded a new religious movement.

        1. Hong came from a Hakka village and was trying to lift his family's fortunes through an official career.

        2. He repeatedly took the entry-level exam and failed each time.

3. He was exposed to Christian missionary tracts during his visits to the examination site in Guangzhou.
4. During a stress-induced illness following one of his examination attempts, he saw visions that he later interpreted as visits from God and Jesus, who was his older brother.
5. He conceived the mission of creating a heavenly kingdom in China.

II. The Taiping Movement grew through the 1840s.
  A. Hong first formed the Society of God Worshippers.
    1. This group formed a kind of rural utopia.
    2. Many of the original members were Hakka, but the movement grew beyond the Hakka community.
    3. Hong had repeated visions and developed his self-centered theology.

  B. As others joined his movement, Hong's ambitions expanded, and he planned a campaign to overthrow the Qing.
    1. Thousands of farmers and artisans flocked to Hong's group.
    2. The Taipings developed an ideology of radical egalitarianism and the communal ownership of land.
    3. They were also extreme sexual puritans, breaking up families and living in single-sex dormitories.
    4. By the end of the decade, they were ready to attack the dynasty.

III. In 1850, the Taipings launched a military campaign to overthrow the Qing.
  A. They set out from Guangdong province and marched north through Hunan to the Yangzi valley.
    1. As they fought their way north, they won repeated battles against the weak and demoralized Qing army.
    2. The gained many converts along the way.
    3. When they reached the Yangzi River, they headed east to Nanjing, where they set up their "Heavenly Capital."

  B. From 1854 to 1864, the Heavenly Kingdom of Great Peace controlled much of central and southern China, with a population of more than 100 million.

1. Although there were some efforts to conquer the north, the movement seems to have stalled out once it captured Nanjing.
2. Hong Xiuquan and his fellow leaders settled into palaces in Nanjing and led a rich life of indulgence while their followers lived in poverty and sexual segregation.
3. The Western powers, which had at first been intrigued with Hong's professed Christianity, decided that he was not sane and declined to support the Taiping.

III. The response of the Qing was slow in coming but eventually resulted in the defeat of the Taipings.

   A. The established Qing military was in disarray.
      1. Elite Manchu banner forces had fallen into decadence and neglect.
      2. Chinese units were poorly paid and undisciplined.
      3. The defeats by the British had demoralized the military.

   B. In the face of early Taiping successes, the Qing turned to local Chinese leaders for help.
      1. One such leader was Zeng Guofan, from Hunan.
      2. Zeng built up a local defense force, funded from a new tax on trade within Hunan province.
      3. The Hunan Army became an effective fighting force, with the latest weapons and decent pay.
      4. Other local forces developed, and these played the decisive role in ending the Taiping Rebellion.

   C. By 1864, the new provincial armies came together to destroy the Taiping regime.
      1. Hong Xiuquan was killed and tens of thousands of Taiping followers were massacred in Nanjing.
      2. The defeat of the Taipings saved the Qing rulers, but the sharing of power with local Chinese leaders changed the political landscape for the rest of the dynasty.
      3. In the wake of defeat by the British and the narrow escape from the Taiping Rebellion, some Chinese leaders began to seek to reform the state, a process we will examine in the next lecture.

Essential Reading:

Jonathan Spence, *God's Chinese Son*.

Supplemental Reading:

Elizabeth J. Perry, *Rebels and Revolutionaries in North China, 1845–1945*.

Questions to Consider:

1. Hong Xiuquan's claim to be the younger brother of Jesus Christ seems absurd to modern Westerners, yet it appealed to tens of millions of Chinese in the 1840s and 1850s. What might have been attractive in such a vision?

2. The Manchus had conquered China two centuries before the Taiping Rebellion and had lost much of their martial vigor, as indicated by the need to raise new armies from the Chinese provinces, yet Manchu rule persisted until the early 20th century. Why were the Manchus able to survive as an alien elite while earlier conquerors, such as the Mongols or the Jurchen, fell in much less time?

Lecture Twenty-Nine—Transcript
The Taiping Heavenly Kingdom

China's defeat by Britain in the Opium War, and the opening of China to greater European influence, greater Western influences with the Treaty of Nanjing and the other treaties that other Western powers signed in the ensuing years, created new circumstances that put a lot of stress on the social life of southern China. Some of this came from the effects of the opium trade, the spread of addiction, but others were related to more fundamental economic causes. The opening of the treaty ports, for example, resulted in the reorientation of traditional trade routes. People who had been involved in the transportation of goods in China's interior were, in some instances, thrown out of work as ports along the coast assumed a greater role in trade, and interior markets were accordingly neglected somewhat. There were a variety of other effects that began to be felt, particularly in southern China, in the wake of these new circumstances.

There were, of course, already plenty of problems within Chinese society, as we've talked about, stemming out of some of the weaknesses in the system—overpopulation, the limits on further economic expansion stemming out of the population growth from the 17th and 18th centuries. Southern China, by the middle of the 19th century, was a place that was in many ways ready for fairly catastrophic events, and they came along quite appropriately. The particular circumstances of south China, because of its geography, because of the way that we've talked about several times, that it's hillier, the population tends to be not spread so smoothly around the region, but concentrated in the lowlands, in the valleys and coastal plain areas.

There were, in certain areas of southern China—particularly the rural parts of Guangdong province, southern parts of Hunan province—local ethnic groups, local populations that had very distinctive cultural traditions; and one of these, not one of the formerly indigenous people, the people who had been displaced by Chinese migration and had moved up into the highlands, but actually people who had migrated from northern China themselves, who were themselves Chinese, but who were seen by their neighbors as different, people who were known as the Hakka, or in Mandarin, the Gejia, the guest families. These were families, northern Chinese families who had moved to the south later on, after the initial waves of Chinese migrants had come south, and they therefore brought with them a culture, a northern culture which was a little different from that which had evolved in local society. They retained that distinctive quality; indeed, they retain a distinctive identity today.

The Hakka people, because they were marginal, summit outsiders in the larger context of south Chinese society, tended to take care of each other, tended to be very self-reliant, but they were affected particularly strongly by some of the consequences of the opening of the treaty ports and of the internal problems that Qing society was facing early in the 19th century, and this made them perhaps more receptive to new ideas, more receptive to unusual ideas, ideas which were not part of the traditional cultural scene in China. An individual appears in south China who presents a really interesting story, who we're going to look at here. I have to put him into a special context because it's unlike anything we've really dealt with thus far. This is a man whose name is Hong Xiuquan.

Hong Xiuquan was himself a Hakka, so he starts off as something of a special situation. He was from a family that was not particularly wealthy, but was well enough off that they had been able to allow him to be educated and to prepare to take the examinations, and his ambition, his hope was that through success in the examinations, he would be able to lift his family fortunes. So, there was a lot invested in him, a lot invested in his education, a lot materially invested, and a lot psychologically invested in this idea that he was going to be in some ways the salvation of his family. He repeatedly took the entry-level examinations to get a start into the Confucian examination system, but each time he sat for the examinations, he failed. He was never successful in passing even the entry-level examinations.

To take these examinations, he would go into the large city of Guangzhou, or Canton as we know it, and when he would be in the city, of course it was a very lively and dynamic city, it was a port city, it was a city where there was a strong Western presence even before the Opium War as the focal point of the trade with foreigners, and it was a city where he encountered people and ideas that were very different, very unfamiliar, very alien. Among the unusual people that he may have encountered in Guangzhou were Christian missionaries, and we know that in fact, during one of his visits to take the exams, he was given a set of writings, of missionary tracts which he didn't apparently pay a lot of attention to immediately, but took home with them, read them through and didn't really understand what all this was about and set them aside. A few years later, during another effort to pass the exams, another unsuccessful effort to pass the exams, he basically exhausted himself. He had studied so hard, worked so hard, and then the stress of the exams was so difficult, and the psychological blow of yet another failure seems to have caused him to have a kind of breakdown. He goes home and takes to his bed. He spent two weeks basically trying to shut the world out.

During that time, he had dreams or visions in which an old gentleman with a long white beard and a younger man with a dark beard appear to him and talked with him. When he recovered from his breakdown, when he was back on his feet, he was reflecting on his dreams or his vision, and he took down these Christian tracts which he had been given years before, and he read through them again and he had a sudden revelation, which was that the old man in the dream, in the vision was God, the young man with the dark beard was Jesus, and that what they had been telling him was that he, Hong Xiuquan, was the younger brother of Jesus, and that is his mission to bring the story of Christianity to the Chinese people. This launches him upon his life's work, and he abandons the idea of trying to pass the Confucian examinations and indeed begins to develop an understanding of the world in which the whole Confucian system, the whole imperial order of China is now seen as something that he has to overcome, something that he must speak out against, something that he must seek to do away with.

He therefore begins to create a movement with himself as the focal point, to establish on earth a heavenly kingdom. This comes to be called the Taiping Tianguo, which means the Heavenly Kingdom of Great Peace. This becomes Hong Xiuquan's mission. At first, in the late 1830s and the beginning of the 1840s, this takes the form of something that he calls the Society of God Worshippers. Many of the people who were initially involved with the Society of God Worshippers were themselves from the Hakka community, but it grew beyond just being identified with this one particular social group. The Hakka are very important in the beginning of the Taiping movement because they give the body of followers with a high degree of social cohesion the Hong Xiuquan can work with when he gets started, but it is always his ambition to take this beyond just being a Hakka-centered phenomenon, and to make it something which is for all the Chinese people. It's clear that right from the start that he has this vision of establishing the heavenly kingdom on earth for all the Chinese people.

Hong Xiuquan continues to have visions. He continues to develop a theological system in which his role as the younger brother of Jesus is the principal feature. As far as we can tell, he never read to the Christian Bible; his understanding of Christianity is almost entirely derived from these few simple missionary tracts, which he had acquired and read through. He does later on undertake some more serious study of Christianity, but he certainly is not a scholar of the church or anything like that. Instead, his appeal is based apparently his own personal charisma. His faith in himself, his belief in his mission was apparently quite compelling, and he attracts around himself a core of followers, some of whom were at well educated, some of whom were fairly well-to-do people, merchants and others like that, even some officials, but the vast majority of his followers of course were ordinary farmers.

They established in rural western Guangdong province, northwest of the great city of Canton, a kind of utopian commune based upon Hong Xiuquan's understanding of the principles of primitive Christian communism. They had a very radical egalitarianism, there were to be no ranks, no hierarchy, which of course was a very thorough break with the Confucian idea of a well-ordered society in which everybody was in a certain hierarchical relationship to one another. For the Taiping, it was a very egalitarian vision. They abolished private property within the commune. Everything was to be shared communally; everything was to be owned in common. Indeed, as time went by, they began they took on some very extreme characteristics. They were sexual puritans. In fact, they segregated men and women so that they lived in separate dormitories. Families were broken up; marriage was seen as part of the traditional Confucian system which needed to be rejected. It was a very thorough, a very comprehensive system for organizing society in ways which, in many ways, inverted the basic principles of the Confucian order.

This apparently had a tremendous appeal because thousands and thousands of people came to take part in this movement, and in the course of the 1840s, it grew and it expanded territorially, and the number of people involved got to be greater and greater. In the course of that, Hong Xiuquan's ambitions also grew, also developed, and he went from simply having a vision of a community that was separate from Chinese society, that was a pure retreat from Chinese society, to taking that movement, taking that community as a base for launching an assault on the existing order and to try and overthrow the Qing dynasty and to establish the Heavenly Kingdom right now, right there on earth, in China. In 1850, they reached the point where it was time to act on these ambitions, and Hong Xiuquan, along with the number of his other leaders—he evolves a system where he is the heavenly king, and then he had four subordinate assistant kings, who represented the different cardinal directions: a king of the east, the north, the south, the west, and they were the governing elite, the central leadership within the Taiping movement as a whole.

Under that leadership, in 1850 they launch a military campaign, and they move from Guangdong province in the far south of China, they start to head north. They fight their way up through central China, through Hunan province, which borders on Guangdong at the south and on the Yangzi River at the north, and so they make their way up through Hunan province. They fight against the armies of the Qing dynasty and defeat them and drive them away. As they go, their appeal to the peasants of Hunan, their appeal to the poor, the marginalized populations of central China, is quite effective, and large numbers of people flock to join the Taiping movement, and as it progresses north, it just gets bigger and bigger as it goes along. When they reach the Yangzi River, they turn east and head downriver until they come to Nanjing, which was a great city, one of the truly great cities of the empire. It had of course been the southern capital during the Ming dynasty and even under the Qing. Although it no longer had the role of being a secondary imperial capital, it was the seat of government for that part of China, and it still had its ancient city walls, it still had the palaces of the former Ming emperors. It was a very wealthy and rich, glorious city.

The Taiping occupy Nanjing and proclaim it to be their heavenly capital; and from 1854, when they finally reach Nanjing, they make it the center of their movement for the next 10 years. During that decade, especially in the first 2-3 years, they continue to fight, to try to expand their territory. They send an expedition to the north that doesn't really succeed very well. It fights its way north, but then turns and heads back south without really reaching the Qing capital at Beijing and returns to Nanjing. They also fight in the area south and east of Nanjing; and indeed, over time the territory that they control shifts around. Initially they have more strength in the west, but later on their control shifts over further to the east.

Once they're in Nanjing, the Heavenly Kingdom undergoes some changes, which proved to be quite problematic. Most particularly, once they occupy this great capital city, Hong Xiuquan and the other kings move into the former imperial palaces, and when they settle in there, they begin to really live a much more imperial kind of life. They eat very well, they have lots of luxuries, and perhaps most significantly, they establish a kind of harem for themselves in the imperial residents. Meanwhile, the vast majority of Taiping followers continue to live in circumstances of Puritanism, egalitarianism and indeed relative poverty. As many as 100 million people seem to have been involved in the Taiping movement at its peak. This was perhaps a quarter of the population of China. They controlled a significant territory, several southern provinces, parts of Jiangsu and Shanxi, Zhejiang province on the coast, Hunan province and Hubei province in central China, at least parts of all these provinces were under Taiping control, so it was geographically a very extensive space and controlled a very large population.

The differential in lifestyle that emerges once they reach Nanjing begins to be a problem. There's some resentment on the part of ordinary members of the Taiping towards this luxurious lifestyle that Hong Xiuquan and the other kings are leading. The enthusiasm of ordinary families, ordinary people for this very austere lifestyle, for the sexual segregation, for the breaking up of families seems to have waned as time went on. It was very difficult to maintain that level of intensity and enthusiasm year after year, particularly once they had settled in with Nanjing as the capital, and once the phase of real active military campaigning had come to an end. So, tensions begin to build up within the Taiping community, within the Taiping kingdom itself. While all this is going on, the dynasty has to respond in some way. The outburst of the Taiping movement in south China, and its march up through Hunan and then its occupation of Nanjing, these are very problematic from the point of view of the government. The Qing dynasty has suffered these great military defeats and humiliations at the hands of the British and the other Western powers, and now they have to deal with this very serious threat from within.

Initially, they're not very effective. The military situation within the country is not good. The Qing dynasty military system had two basic components. On the one hand, what were called the banners—and this was the military system of the Manchus themselves, which they had built up before the conquest, had been the system they used in conquering China—Manchu banners were not solely composed of Manchu people. There were Chinese and Mongol and other ethnic members within the banner system, but the banner troops were the elite troops. Then there were also what was called the green standard army, which were the ordinary Chinese troops, and there were many more of these then there were of the banner forces. Both the banner forces and the green standard army by the 1850s were not in very good shape. They weren't very well trained, discipline wasn't very high, and they weren't very well equipped. Many of the banner troops hadn't seen action in over a century. They tended to preserve their traditions, but not very well. The green standard army hadn't been used extensively since the suppression of Wu Sangui's rebellion back in the 1670s and early 1680s, so these were not military organizations in their fighting prime, and they melted away to a large extent as the Taiping made their way north.

The dynasty then had to find a way to make a more effective response. What they did was to turn to a new source of organization and a new source of support for military activities. What they wound up doing, and this becomes very significant politically, even after the Taipings are suppressed, was to turn to local Chinese elites. As we've seen in the past, going all the way back certainly to the Song dynasty and in many ways even prior to that, the local elites, the literati in their capacity as the wealthy families in local communities, performed a lot of quasi-governmental functions, and these often included providing local kinds of security, perhaps local militias, anti-bandit activities, things like that. Now the Qing state decides to appeal to local leaders to assume a greater role in what they're arguing is basically local self-defense. The classic example of this is a man called Zeng Guofan.

Zeng Guofan was from Hunan province, which had been the province that the Taiping had marched through and which the imperial military had been completely unable to defend. Zeng

Guofan is given the responsibility on the one hand—but also the authority by the Qing government—to organize local troops, to come up with some new way to put together an effective military force in central China. Most significantly, or most hopefully, he's also given a new financial basis to do this on. Part of a problem with the banner troops and the green standard army is that they're not paid very well; there are not resources in the imperial treasuries to support them. Zeng Guofan is given control over a new source of revenue, and this is what's called the *lijin*, which is a tariff on trade, on local trade. If goods are moving about within Hunan province, or into the province, or out of the province, at various border stations very modest tariffs are collected. But Hunan is a very wealthy province; it's a province where there's a lot of trade going on. It's a big tea-growing province, a rice-exporting province, and so there's a fair manner of trade to be cashed, and the lijin becomes a news source of revenue.

The revenue that's generated through these tariffs is put into Zeng Guofan's hands. They say, "Here's your funds, use these, do something to put these Taiping down." Zeng Guofan proves to be more than equal to the task, and he takes these resources, he recruits soldiers, he hires professionals to help train them, and very quickly he puts together what comes to be called, not surprisingly, the Hunan Army. Other local leaders in other parts of central China also get involved in this process. Zeng Guofan is perhaps the best known and in some ways the theoretician of all this. He writes a lot about it; his writings are still very popular in China, even today. He equips the Hunan Army with the latest kinds of weaponry. He pays them well, clothes them well, feeds them well, they're very well disciplined, and he then begins, towards the end of the 1850s, beginning of the 1860s, to deploy them in campaigns directed against the Taiping Heavenly Kingdom.

The Western powers also have an interesting role in all of this. The treaty ports that are opened in the wake of the Treaty of Nanjing in the Opium War are along the south China coast. The most northerly of them is Shanghai, which, when it is open as a treaty port, is a relatively obscure fishing village, but grows quite quickly since it's the treaty port closest to the mouth of the Yangzi River, grows quite quickly to be a very large city. By the time that the Taiping rebellion is in full swing, and by the time the Taiping are occupying Nanjing, although it's only been about a decade since Shanghai is opened as a treaty port, it has already grown to have a significant Western presence. It becomes, in a sense, the capital of the Europeans in China. The Europeans find themselves in an interesting situation because Hong Xiuquan claims to be a Christian. He presents his rebellion as a Christian movement. He is, of course, Jesus' younger brother, so he appeals to the Westerners in many ways as a figure that might be easier to deal with, that might be better to deal with than the Qing government. The Qing government are, after all, heathens, non-Christians, barbarians, however you want to think of them, and so there's an interest on the part of at least some in the Western community about what's going on with this Heavenly Kingdom, with this Hong Xiuquan.

They send a diplomatic delegation to Nanjing that meets with the Taiping leadership, and the result of this is that they come to see Hong Xiuquan not as someone that can be allied with, not as someone that can be really integrated into the Christian community, but they come to see him basically as a lunatic, as someone who has delusions and who is claiming a divine status for himself. Of course, this is not really going to work very well with established Christian teachings and doctrine. The Western powers do not decide to rally to the support of the Taiping, and indeed, after some reflection, they decide that their interests are best served by sustaining the role of the Qing state, and so there's some Western military intervention in support of the Qing government.

In 1864, the Taiping kingdom finally falls. Zeng Guofan's army defeats and destroys the last remnants of the Heavenly Kingdom. There are great massacres when Nanjing is taken; and in other places, great battles are fought and won by the Qing, and the rebellion, which was only one of a number of challenges, but certainly the greatest, the most dynamic one in the middle of the 19th century of domestic rebellions in China, is put down, is brought to an end. By this time, the West has established its position quite firmly. The Qing state now is something which the Western powers want to preserve and maintain. The role, minimal as it may have been in the suppression of the Taiping, is significant. The Chinese now have to decide, and the Manchu rulers have to decide where they're going from here. How can they respond to the continued presence of the West, the continued threat that that implies? We'll see some of the efforts that they make in the next lecture.

Lecture Thirty
Efforts at Reform

Scope:

The humiliation of the Opium War and the challenge of the Taiping Rebellion left a deep impression on the Qing leadership. In the second half of the 19th century, efforts were undertaken to reform the dynasty and adapt Western ideas and technologies to strengthen China and give it the ability to resist Western domination. Although they achieved some successes, these measures ultimately proved inadequate. China was again defeated militarily in 1894–1895 by the Japanese, whose aggressive adoption of Western ways contrasted strongly with the general conservatism of China. A final wave of reformist activity, with the support of the Guangxu emperor in the summer of 1898, was thwarted by the Empress Dowager Cixi and was followed by the anti-foreign Boxer Rebellion of 1899–1900. Western troops invaded China to suppress the Boxers and again imposed harsh humiliations on the tottering Manchu regime.

Outline

I.   In the wake of the Opium War and the Taiping Rebellion, some Chinese and Manchus began to pursue reform.

   A. Even before the final suppression of the Taipings, there were efforts to revive the Qing.

      1. In the 1860s, during the reign of the young Tongzhi emperor, progressive senior officials sought to restore vitality to the court.

      2. As new leaders, such as Zeng Guofan, emerged in provincial activities, they were offered roles in reform.

   B. In the 1870s and 1880s, the Self-Strengthening Movement sought to modernize the Qing state and military.

      1. Chinese officials undertook initiatives to develop a modern weapons industry, including building shipyards and arsenals.

      2. A bureau for translating Western books, especially on science and technology, was founded.

      3. The Zongli Yamen, a kind of foreign ministry, was set up to handle relations with the Western powers.

C. Despite these efforts, China continued to be treated as an inferior by foreign states.

    1. In 1884, China was defeated by France as the French established their control over Vietnam, a client state of China's.

    2. In 1894–1895, China suffered a severe embarrassment when Japan inflicted a crushing defeat on both land and sea, ending Chinese influence in Korea.

II. The defeat of 1895 set off a new, more intense round of reform.

    A. In the autumn of 1895, examination candidates in Beijing demonstrated in protest over China's weakness.

        1. A minor official, Kang Youwei, organized a petition drive to call for government reform.

        2. Others, including Liang Qichao, began to write articles advocating political change.

    B. In 1898, the Guangxu emperor embraced reform and issued a series of edicts.

        1. He called for modernizing the educational system and studying Western, as well as Chinese, topics.

        2. He wanted to streamline administration and reduce bureaucracy.

        3. He wanted to increase opportunities for people to communicate with the government.

        4. He appointed several reformers to high positions.

    C. Many senior Manchus feared that reform would weaken their power, and these "100 Days," as they were known, were brought to an abrupt end.

        1. The Manchu nobles worried that Chinese officials would move to eliminate their influence and, perhaps, to terminate rule by the Manchu minority.

        2. Some Chinese officials also feared reform and allied with the conservative Manchus.

        3. The Empress Dowager Cixi resented the autonomy of her nephew, the emperor, and moved to block his changes.

        4. In September 1898, she ordered the arrest of eight leading reformers, who were executed shortly thereafter.

        5. Kang Youwei and Liang Qichao fled to exile in Japan.

III. The thwarting of reform allowed popular anti-foreign feelings to overflow in the Boxer Rebellion.

  A. The Boxers were members of a martial arts movement with mystical beliefs.

    1. Centered in Shandong province, the Boxers were angered by the privileges of foreign missionaries and the favors given to Chinese Christian converts.

    2. They also resented the special concessions Germany held at Qingdao.

    3. Boxer fighters believed certain talismans would protect them from Western firearms.

    4. They thought that divine spirits would come to save China from the "barbarians."

  B. In 1899, the Boxers moved out of Shandong and headed toward Beijing.

    1. They began to receive official approval.

    2. In June, they besieged the Western diplomatic legations in the capital.

    3. An international force, led by Russian and Japanese troops, fought its way into Beijing and lifted the siege in August.

    4. The Western powers occupied Beijing and imposed a harsh settlement on the Chinese, thus ending the last challenge to Western power under imperial rule.

    5. The days of the Qing dynasty were now numbered; we will follow the course of its fall in the next lecture.

Essential Reading:

Paul A. Cohen and John Schrecker, *Reform in Nineteenth Century China*.

Supplemental Reading:

Benjamin Schwartz, *In Search of Wealth and Power*.

Joseph W. Esherick, *The Origins of the Boxer Uprising*.

Questions to Consider:

1. In the middle decades of the 19th century, the Japanese managed to completely transform their government and military in line with contemporary Western models. Why was reform so difficult in China?

2. Chinese reformers wanted to adopt Western technologies and administrative practices but resisted the embrace of Western values. Was this a reasonable response on their part?

Lecture Thirty—Transcript
Efforts at Reform

China's defeat in the Opium War, and then the trauma of the great Taiping rebellion in the middle of the 19th century, shook the foundations of the Qing dynasty quite profoundly. The dynasty survived both these challenges, but it knew—or at least some within the leadership knew—that if China wanted to flourish again, if China wanted to ever reclaim a more upright position in the community of nations, that some sort of change was going to have to take place. In the years from the 1860s through the early 1890s, certain leaders, both within the Chinese and the Manchu elites, began to pursue a program designed to give China the ability to stand up to Western powers, to not have to simply accept the humiliations of economic dependency—of the treaties, the unequal treaties as they came to be called, the doctrines such as extraterritoriality, under which foreigners were not subject to Chinese law—but only to their own regulation.

This movement from the 1860s through the early 1890s, comes to be called the "Self-Strengthening Movement;" the idea being that China couldn't rely on outsiders, couldn't rely on the foreign powers to take care of it—they obviously were pursuing their own interests, which were often antithetical to those of China—if China wished to be strong enough to assume control of its own destiny, they had to strengthen themselves; and so, the Self-Strengthening Movement is the response of some leaders within the Chinese government to these challenges. The 1860s was a time when it was possible to make some changes in China, in the Qing government, because a young emperor had come to the throne in 1860. Being young, he was subject to a regency, a council of his elders who guided his reign, and those elders among them were some officials who were very receptive to the need for new solutions to the problems China was facing. The leaders, like Zeng Guofan that we mentioned in the last lecture—who became a military reformer and put together the Hunan Army that was so critical in the suppression of the Taiping movement—and other provincial leaders amongst the Chinese emerged in the course of the Self-Strengthening Movement to really provide the brains of an effort to get China back on its own feet.

The 1870s and 1880s, are really the core of the Self-Strengthening period. During that time, the Chinese undertook a number of fairly diverse initiatives to try to improve their situation. On one hand, they recognized that the superior position of the West was largely founded simply on military strength. The British in the Opium War in 1839-42 had not really met serious resistance from the Chinese. The superiority of British weapons, the superiority of British naval vessels was so clear that the Chinese realized that—the Self-Strengthening leaders realized—they were going to have to find a way to counter them, and the way to do that was to develop their own modern military sector. Part of the way they went about this was to simply try to buy ships and equipment from the Western powers. But they recognized that even that was not enough. If they really wanted to develop a sense of self-reliance, if they really wanted China to be able to advance on the military front, they had to be responsible for their own armaments.

The British, who sold the Chinese a number of warships and other military systems in the second half of the 19th century, were always very careful to make sure that the equipment that they sold was outdated and often obsolete from their own military perspective. They were willing to sell it off to the Chinese, knowing that it would not be equal to the equipment that they themselves were currently putting a field. If the Chinese wanted to keep up with, to try to catch up with the British in any way, they were going to have to do this on the basis of their own resources. Accordingly, they established a great arsenal and a great shipyard, the shipyard near the mouth of the Yangzi River, the arsenal near the central Chinese city of Hankou, which is part of the much larger urban area of Wuhan today, also on the Yangzi River. The arsenal at Wuhan was also near sources of coal and iron ore so that they were able to begin the process of developing a steel industry as well, which initially was designed to supply military needs, but eventually extended beyond that as well.

Developing a modern Western-style military was one priority for the Self-Strengthening move reformers; a second, which was certainly not unrelated, had to do with learning about Western science and technology. This was of course fundamental to successfully opening and operating these industries and armaments, factories and things like that, but there was a recognition that Western superiority went beyond just the military field. There was an understanding of sorts about the nature of industrial production in Europe, particularly in England, and a sense that Western science gave to the imperialist powers part of the strength that allowed them to dominate China.

The Qing government set up a bureau for translating Western books and publishing them, and circulating them amongst the educated elite in China. Initially, these were focused primarily on very practical books, books about science and technology, but after a large number of those had been translated, they also began to look at works on social science, works on political theory, and particularly they became particularly interested with a lot of the Western writing at this time that we can associate with the idea of social Darwinism, the idea that societies, that nations compete, and that international relations was in some ways a kind of survival of the best. Of course, this fit in nicely with the thinking of the Self-Strengthening reformers, because what they wanted to do was make China fitter in the competition for survival.

Finally, a third dimension of the Self-Strengthening Movement was a realization that there was a need to restructure the way that China related to other countries in the world. The international order which the Qing dynasty was used a functioning in, and which had been the norm for previous dynasties, was one in which China was at the center and other countries generally were expected to come and pay their respects. It's often referred to as the "tribute system." Delegations from countries around China would come to the capital and pay their respects to the emperor and offer various kinds of tribute goods, and the emperor would then give them very rich presents that they would take back to their country, and this was seen as the normal pattern of relations, where other countries paid homage and respect to China. Obviously, this wasn't working with the Western powers, and China was forced to pay homage and respect to the British and the French and the Americans and all the other Western powers.

They recognize though that amongst the Western powers, there was a system which was supposedly based on equality among nations. The very concept of treaties between nations is based on the idea that both parties are equal, that they sign these agreements, these are essentially contracts between nations, and so they should be signed between equal parties. The real content of the treaties that were in place in the 19th century were unequal. They were dictated, the terms were dictated by the power of the Western countries, and China simply had to basically accept whatever was offered to them. But they realized that the rhetoric at least of international law, of international relations was one that was based upon diplomatic relations amongst equal partners. To give China the ability to participate more fully in that system, they created a new institutional structure for China's international relations, which was focused on what's called the Zongli Yamen. The Zongli Yamen was a foreign ministry, and that was the governmental body which then became responsible for handling diplomatic interaction with the Western powers.

These efforts were certainly very sincere and pursued quite assiduously by their advocates, but they were really not sufficient to solve the problems that China was confronted with. For one thing, the self-strengtheners—although many of the leading officials in China at the time participated in the movement—were never a real majority. They were never the dominant group within the imperial bureaucracy, or even within the councils of state at the capital. They were prestigious, they were certainly successful individuals within the imperial system; but as a movement, they never came to be the real mainstream of Chinese policy. Resistance to modernization was perhaps more characteristic of the conservative majority amongst Chinese officials. So, there were efforts to undermine the position of the self-strengtheners, there were efforts to preserve the old ways of very classic bureaucratic mentality, "We don't want to do new things; we don't want to try new approaches because this is the way things have always been done," and there was certainly plenty of that mentality within the Chinese and Manchu elites.

The insufficiency of the Self-Strengthening Movement begins to be demonstrated in the mid-1880s, when China was defeated in a war with France. France was at this point attempting to establish—and indeed, were successful in establishing—their control over Indochina. Vietnam in particular had always been a close ally, almost a dependency of China, and they appealed to China, to the Qing, to defend them against the French. The Chinese did indeed send part of their modernized navy down to the Gulf of Tonkin, but the French defeated them, and this was a further humiliation and certainly a setback for the Self-Strengtheners. Ten years later, the failures of the Self-Strengthening Movement really were most clearly revealed in a war between China and Japan.

Without going into the details of the history of Japan at this time, suffice it to say that when Japan had been forcibly opened by the Western powers, by the United States, in the 1850s, they had decided to embark upon a campaign of modernization in a thoroughgoing, all-out kind of way. The Meiji Restoration in the late 1860s set the Japanese on a course of out-and-out modernization, industrialization, Westernization. By the end of the 19th century, they had gone a long way to achieving those objectives. They had developed their economy, developed their military, and established their position in the system of international relations, almost on a par with that of the great Western powers. This was demonstrated in the war of 1894-1895, which was fought largely in Korea over issues of who was going to control Korea, but in the course of which, the Japanese simply inflicted one defeat after another on the Chinese. On land, they defeated the modernized forces of the Chinese army; and at sea, they were successful in destroying much of the modern component of the Chinese fleet.

The Sino-Japanese War, as it's called, was an even greater humiliation for China. It was one thing to be defeated by the Europeans; they were barbarians, yes, but they were foreign strangers. No one really knew much about them prior to the Opium War. There was almost a disdain on the part of the Chinese to learn that much about these Europeans, until they had to be taken seriously based on their military strike. The Japanese were very familiar, and had always been seen as little brothers, as junior partners in the cultural system of East Asia. To have the Japanese now inflict this kind of military humiliation on China was very dispiriting, to say the least. In fact, the defeat, which was finalized in a treaty, the Treaty of Shimonoseki in 1895, triggers a protest movement in China. Candidates for the imperial examinations assembling at the capital in Beijing circulate a petition, which gets several thousand signatures, and is submitted to the court demanding that a more effective response to imperialist aggression be made.

Leaders of this movement, in particular a man named Kang Youwei, and another, Liang Qichao worked very closely together, began to write articles, began to publish newspapers, and wrote memorials to the throne. Both Kang and Liang had passed the examinations and were minor officials and had the right to submit memorials to the throne, and other officials in other parts of China joined them in this as well. They advocated that the Qing government adopt a more authoritarian program of reform, not just of piecemeal modernization, but also of complete institutional restructuring to give China a more effective modern-style government, in some ways along the lines of what the Japanese had been doing since the Meiji Restoration.

In 1898, after three years of agitation around these themes, the reformers got a chance to put their ideas into action. The emperor at that time, known as the Guangxu emperor, had come to the throne as a very young man and had been dominated by his ancestor, the Empress Dowager Cixi, a very famous and powerful woman in Chinese history. But in the early 1890s, Cixi had retired from the day-to-day oversight of the courts and had allowed Guangxu to assume more responsibility for managing the affairs of state. In 1898, Guangxu is convinced by the arguments of the reformers that it's necessary to save China, to embark on a program of fairly radical reform, and from the middle of June to the middle of September 1898, we have what comes to be called the "100 Days," the 100 Days of Reform.

In this period, Guangxu listened to the advice of a number of his officials. He received further ideas from Kang Youwei and Liang Qichao and others, and he issued a series of edicts designed to streamline administration, to reduce bureaucracy, to open up the channels for popular input so he could know more about what was going on in the empire and what the desires and aspirations of ordinary people were. He appointed a number of the advocates of reform to high positions, including in the Grand Council, and appeared to be quite well embarked upon a process of transforming the machinery of the imperial state. But, as with the Self-Strengtheners, there were many people in the Qing establishment who were uncomfortable, who were quite resistant to the 100 Days reforms, and who either simply ignored them, passively sat things out waiting to see how things would really develop, or actively resisted them, simply refused to implement them or conspired to try to undermine the reformers.

Eventually, in mid-September, conservative Manchu officials and some Chinese officials, in particular a man named Yuan Shikai—who was, ironically, another commander of the modern troops within the Chinese army and who had decided that the reforms had gone too far—they, along with Cixi, the empress dowager, resolved to put an end to this, to put a stop to this. Accordingly, the emperor was effectively placed under house arrest; the leading reformers were rounded up. Eight of them were executed. Kang Youwei and Liang

Qichao managed to get tipped off and fled Beijing, made their way to Shanghai, eventually to Japan, and the reforms were brought to a complete halt. This ended what had been perhaps the last best hope for getting the Qing dynasty onto a course of modernization, which might have given it the capacity to enter into a modern political era, an era where it could've remained as the effective government and leadership of China. But by terminating the reforms, by bringing this process to an abrupt and violent end, Cixi had signaled that a more conservative orientation, a more traditional orientation was going to remain dominant.

While these events were transpiring in the capital, other things had been going on out in provincial life which now began to come together with high level elite politics and really brings about a very violent conclusion to the 19th century and sets the stage for the final collapse of the dynasty. This is what we know as the Boxer Rebellion. The Boxer Rebellion is in many ways part of a long tradition of popular peasant movements in Chinese history, in Chinese society. If we go all the way back to the Han dynasty, we talked a little bit about the peasant rebellions late in the second century that were part of the collapse of the Han, similar movements were involved in the fall of many dynasties as the course of Chinese history progressed. Often, these popular movements were religious in nature, or had a strong spiritual component, and that is certainly the case with the Boxers.

The name that we use for this group, we call them the Boxers, is based upon the fact that it arises from, and their leaders certainly were involved in, a martial arts school, a martial arts movement. They believed that by practicing certain kinds of exercises, spiritual exercises and physical exercises, they would make themselves invulnerable. They would assume supernatural powers, and bullets fired from the guns of the Westerners would not, for example, hurt them. This was a movement that spread quite rapidly. It had its center in the Western part of Shangdong province, a little southeast of the capital. This was an area that had its own very particular circumstances. It was an area that was relatively poor. It was an area where popular peasant movements had arisen many times in the past, earlier in the 19th century, and it was an area also where there was a very strong foreign presence. The Germans in particular had acquired concessions in Shangdong province at the city of Qingdao, which of course is where they establish a brewery, which is still very popular today.

But the German presence in Shangdong went far beyond Qingdao, and indeed there were many German missionaries in the interior of Shangdong province, and this fed into a number of problems in local society. The missionaries were seen as aliens, as foreigners intruding into China; but Chinese who converted to Christianity, who took up the Christian message, were also seen as problematic in local society. For one thing, some Chinese became Christians perhaps not out of a completely sincere religious experience, but because there were material benefits to be gained, benefits in terms of access to charity, access to food supplies sometimes—these people were often disparaged as "rice Christians" by their neighbors—but also protection. The missionaries were under the protection of the Qing government, under the terms of the treaties, and often Christians, Chinese Christians would use their affiliation with this foreign religion to gain an advantage in lawsuits or other kinds of disputes in local society, so there was a lot of resentment, a lot of tension that focused on the presence of German missionaries.

The Boxers took it upon themselves to basically purify their communities, to purify their society. They were pretty much localized in western Shangdong to begin with, but they had the sense of being part of a great national empire-wide movement or mission to free China from the domination and control of the foreign barbarians. Initially, the Boxers directed part of their antipathy towards representatives of the Qing government, because the Qing government, under the terms of the treaties, protected the Christian missionaries and Chinese Christians. The Qing government was seen as perhaps being equally part of the problem. Especially after the suppression of the reforms of 1898, the Qing government began to change its tune and began to be more sympathetic, more encouraging to movements like the Boxers, and the governor of Shangdong province made a number of proclamations, "The Boxers aren't such a bad thing, and we should support and encourage their patriotic spirits," he wouldn't have used those terms, but that kind of idea.

By 1898, that encouragement led the Boxers to step up their activities, and they became a much more aggressive and dynamic movement; and as they did so, they also began to attract larger and larger numbers of followers. In the winter of 1899-1900, they moved out of Shangdong province and began to make their way north towards Tianjin. Tianjin was a great treaty port southeast of Beijing; and eventually, by the summer of 1900, they marched on the imperial capital. They entered into the capital; they were well received. The imperial army did not try to keep them out or inhibit their activity; and indeed, the Empress Dowager Cixi, who was now firmly in control of the government, proclaimed that she was on the side of the Boxers. The Boxers began to confront the Westerners that they found in Beijing; and by June of 1900, they laid siege to the diplomatic quarter, or the legation quarter in the eastern side of the city of Beijing, where all the foreign countries had their diplomatic missions.

This siege lasted for some 55 days, and was only lifted when an international military force, with components from eight different countries—including, most interestingly perhaps, Japan, which was now seen as an equal partner with the other imperialist powers—fought their way from Tianjin, up along the railway line and entered Beijing at the middle of August and were able to defeat the boxers and relieve the siege of the diplomatic quarter. The Western powers then occupied Beijing. The emperor and the empress dowager fled and ran away from the capital. This was, of course, yet another tremendous humiliation. The mystical power of the Boxers to resist foreign weapons proved to be completely meaningless. There was no substance to that, of course, and this left the Qing state once more prostrate before the Western powers. A treaty is signed to allow the Qing government to resume its activities, the empress dowager and the emperor are to come back to the capital, and certain Chinese government leaders who had supported the Boxers were executed. Of course, many of the Boxers were killed, and under the terms of what comes to be known as the Boxer Protocol, China was forced to pay an indemnity to the Western powers. Large amounts of money, which they could ill afford and which they had to draw from their maritime customs receipts, the maritime customs were themselves administered by foreign officials, so it was just a really terrible set of blows to the dignity of the dynasty.

It pretty much signaled that the Qing state was no longer really a viable, workable government for China. The days of the dynasty were pretty clearly numbered; it lasted just about another decade, but during that decade, new alternative ideas about China's future became much more influential and much more significant.

Revolutionary movements designed to overthrow the entire imperial heritage and establish a modern form of government for China were waiting in the wings. We'll see the drama of how that story unfolds in our next lecture.

Lecture Thirty-One
The Fall of the Empire

Scope:

The failures of reform efforts gave rise to more radical forces, and agitation for the overthrow of the imperial system grew through the 1890s and the first decade of the 20th century. The revolutionary movement to create a Chinese republic was led by Sun Yatsen and had broad support among educated Chinese who wanted to save their country through modernization. In 1911, a military mutiny led to the collapse of the Qing dynasty, and China appeared to be on the way to a republican system. But corrupt military strongmen soon subverted this process, and by the middle of the 1910s, China descended into a decade of fragmentation, as warlords carved up the former empire into local satrapies.

Outline

I. Shocked by the occupation of Beijing after the Boxer uprising, the Qing made last-minute gestures toward reform, but these efforts were too little and came too late.

   A. The dynasty developed a plan to modernize its administration and to move toward a constitutional monarchy.

   1. In 1905, the Confucian examination system, which had operated without significant interruption since 1380 and with origins going back more than 2,000 years, was abolished.

   2. Many reforms based on the model of 1898 were put into place.

   3. A blueprint for a transition to a constitutional monarchy was developed, with provincial assemblies to begin meeting by 1916.

   B. These measures, however, were not enough to restore faith in the Qing among educated, politically engaged Chinese.

   1. Even in the 1890s, some had begun to advocate outright overthrow of the imperial system.

   2. Anti-Manchu sentiment blended with anti-Western nationalism to spark interest in a revolutionary program of modernization.

II. Sun Yatsen emerged as the principal leader of revolutionary activity.

    A. Sun was from Guangdong province in the south.

        1. He had been educated in Hawaii and Hong Kong and became a doctor of Western medicine.

        2. In the 1880s, he began to think about radical change for China.

        3. He began to build a movement in the 1890s, aimed not at reform but at ending imperial rule.

    B. By the beginning of the 20th century, Sun's movement grew into the mainstream of revolutionary activity.

        1. He founded the *Tongmeng hui*, the Revolutionary League, to bring together various anti-Qing movements.

        2. He traveled extensively in China and around the world, raising money and promoting the ideal of a republican government for China.

        3. Several abortive uprisings were organized by the revolutionaries, but all ended in failure.

III. In 1911, the dynasty collapsed suddenly.

    A. The Empress Dowager and the Guangxu emperor had died in 1908.

        1. A little boy, Puyi, came to the throne as the last emperor.

        2. Conservative Manchu elders slowed down the process of reform.

    B. The modernized military became a focus of revolutionary politics.

        1. Qing efforts to build a modern army had unintended consequences: Officers and men wanted political reform as well.

        2. Junior officers often joined the Revolutionary Alliance.

    C. A mutiny at Wuhan triggered the collapse of the dynasty.

        1. In October 1911, revolutionary soldiers in Wuhan, in central China, feared arrest and seized their garrison.

        2. They proclaimed the surrounding province of Hubei independent of the dynasty.

        3. Over the next weeks, a dozen other provinces declared independence.

D. In the winter of 1911–1912, events moved quickly.

    1. Sun Yatsen, who had been on a speaking tour in America when the revolution broke out, returned to China at the end of the year.

    2. Yuan Shikai, commander of the modern Beiyang Army, negotiated the abdication of the last emperor.

    3. In a political deal, Sun yielded the presidency of the new Republic of China to Yuan.

    4. A provisional assembly was elected in 1912, with Sun's newly formed *Guomindang*, or Nationalist Party, gaining the most seats.

IV. Yuan Shikai betrayed the revolution and precipitated an era of warlordism.

    A. Yuan refused to follow the new constitution and tried to hold on to power.

        1. He dissolved the assembly when it would not support him.

        2. He had a Nationalist leader, Song Jiaoren, assassinated.

        3. He even tried to have himself made emperor.

        4. These efforts failed as a result of rivalry with other warlords. Yuan died in 1916.

    B. Local military leaders then carved China into warlord domains and plunged the country into chaos.

        1. Warfare between militarists caused economic disruption and great suffering among the people.

        2. China's weakness opened the door to Japan's growing ambitions in China, which we will consider in a later lecture.

        3. As the political world fell apart, many Chinese thinkers and activists were seeking new ways to come to grips with the crises they found around them. We will look at this process in the next lecture.

Essential Reading:

Marie-Claire Bergere, *Sun Yat-sen*.

Supplemental Reading:

Joseph W. Esherick, *Reform and Revolution in China*.

Questions to Consider:

1. In abolishing the examination system in 1905, the Qing destroyed the central cultural institution of the literati elite. How did they expect to retain the loyalty of educated Chinese without this?

2. In presenting his revolutionary program in the form of modern nationalism, how might Sun Yatsen have dealt with the problem of Chinese ethnic identity? Could Manchus be Nationalists, too?

Lecture Thirty-One—Transcript
The Fall of the Empire

The crushing of the Boxer Rebellion and the treaty that was imposed upon China in its wake were in some ways the last of the series of humiliations that the Western powers were able to impose upon the Qing dynasty. The shock from this final blow was sufficient to rally even the more conservative members of the Qing elite to a realization that something had to be done if they wanted to preserve their position, that they needed to make changes, which they didn't particularly like, they didn't particularly find to be attractive, but which they came to finally realize were simply a matter of survival. The final decade of the dynasty is one in which reforms are adopted, one after another, which would have been unthinkable—and clearly, had been unthinkable—for these same leaders only a few years earlier.

Perhaps the most remarkable of these comes in 1905, when the Confucian examination system is abolished. The examination system had been operating pretty much without interruption since 1380, and had its origins, its roots well over 2,000 years prior to its abolition. It had been perhaps most important institution, the most important cultural apparatus within China's political system, within the intellectual life of the educated elite, for over 1,000 years; and to have it simply be swept away as a political gesture in 1905, was a very dramatic event.

Many of the reforms that had been proposed, and adopted, and then rescinded in 1898, were now once again put into place. A blueprint for transforming the Qing state from an absolute monarchy into a constitutional monarchy, to create organs of political consultation and participation for new elite sectors in the cities and ports, as well as the traditional land-based literati elite, was developed, and a plan was adopted to create provincial assemblies which would actually begin to function by about 1916. These measures, however, were not really sufficient to the situation. They were developed and began to be implemented in the years between 1901 and 1908, but even at that time, there were already many in China who felt that reforming the dynastic system was no longer the question, and that what was really necessary was to begin to seek some kinds of more radical transformation, to put Chinese society, to put Chinese political life on a non-imperial basis, a non-traditional basis, and indeed, to adopt

Western-style political systems and political ideas to bring China into the modern world.

Interestingly, at this time we get a revival of anti-Manchu ideas. The Manchus had been the rulers of China since the conquest in 1644. I mentioned when we talked about the Qing conquest, the siege of Yangzhou and the massacre that takes place after the city is captured. Beginning around the 1890s, the story of the siege of Yangzhou begins to resurface, begins to be reprinted and circulated in political circles, and a sense that the Manchu conquerors are in part responsible for the weakness of China, that doing away with the alien regime, as it comes to be called, is part of what's necessary to free China to be able to respond effectively to the challenge of modernity. This becomes part of the political discourse, and certainly on the agenda of many. It blends with the broader anti-Western, anti-imperialist nationalism that was also growing during these years.

One individual emerges as perhaps the most representative figure in the quest for a radical alternative, a revolutionary solution to the problems facing China, and this is Sun Yatsen. Sun Yatsen even today remains a very popular figure, often referred to as the father of modern China. You'll see portraits of him in public places, not only in Taiwan, where the political organizations that he had founded continue to be dominant, but even on the mainland, even in other, Communist regimes, Sun Yatsen is seen as the great national hero. Sun Yatsen was actually born in the far south in Guangdong province, near Hong Kong. He was educated partially in Hong Kong, partially in Hawaii, which at that time was still an independent kingdom. His brother lived in Hawaii and Sun, as a young man, spent time there living with his brother and going to school.

In the 1880s, Sun Yatsen began to be attracted to ideas of radical change. By virtue of having a position in both the traditional culture of China and a great exposure to the ideas of the West that he saw both in the British colony of Hong Kong and in Hawaii—which although still an independent country, certainly had shown cultural influences from America and Britain—he came to believe that the imperial system held China back, and that a republic, a modern Western-style republican system, would be the solution needed to put China on the path of modernization. In the 1890s, he began to build a political movement, an avowedly revolutionary movement aiming not to reform and adapt to the institutions of the imperial state, but to abolish them and replace them. After the defeat of China in the Sino-Japanese war in 1895, the failure of the reform movement in 1898, and the further debacle of the Boxer Rebellion in 1899 and 1900, Sun's ideas began to become more and more popular. Many young Chinese, educated Chinese, turned away from the efforts to salvage what they saw as the moribund regime of the Qing and saw Sun's ideas of a revolutionary transformation of China as the way to go, as the more attractive option.

He puts together in the first decade of the 20th century an umbrella organization called the *Tongmeng hui*, or the Revolutionary League, which brought anti-Qing groups with a range of ideas, with a range of particular political perspectives together to strengthen them by giving them a common focus and a common program. He traveled extensively within China and increasingly outside China, around the world, speaking in public, speaking to overseas Chinese communities and raising money. He was apparently a very effective communicator, did a very good job of political agitation and propaganda, and was a first-rate fundraiser. He probably made, in some ways, his major contributions by raising money to support various kinds of revolutionary activities. Some of those revolutionary activities took the form of military uprisings, or at least violent popular uprisings against Qing government officials in various parts of China, particularly in the far south. None of these, however, was successful. They all were rather botched efforts; and the reputation of the Nationalist movement, the revolutionary movement was certainly not as a highly effective rebel organization or terrorist group, but rather more a political movement. All these efforts to spark a popular rebellion, which would overthrow the dynasty, ended in failure.

In 1911, however, the dynasty does collapse, and the way that this comes about was rather particular. The efforts of reform, which had been put in place in the wake of the Boxer Rebellion, begin to stall out after 1908. In 1908, both the Guangxu emperor and the emperor's dowager, Cixi, die. In fact, they die within just a few hours of each other, the Guangxu emperor the evening before the death of the Empress Dowager Cixi. As a result of this, a little boy named Puyi is placed on the throne, and he becomes the last of the Qing emperors—made famous by Bertolucci's film of that name, *The Last Emperor*. As a little boy, he didn't exercise any actual political authority, and his conservative uncles, who constituted a regency council for him, slowed down the reform program, which

Cixi had been presiding over. As a result of this, even the minimal progress that the Qing had been making towards sustaining itself through political adaptation comes to a halt, and the dynasty becomes enters into a final period of rigidity.

Within the dynastic system however, there is one sector where modernization, particularly modern ideas, are becoming increasingly powerful, and this is the military. The military had been the subject of a lot of efforts by the Self-Strengtheners in the 1870s and 1880s and into the early 1890s, and even after the defeat of the modern Chinese army by the Japanese in 1895, there were still efforts made to develop a modern sector in the Chinese military. Again, after the Boxer Rebellion, after the eight-power imperialist army comes into China in 1900. When it's withdrawn in 1901, the Chinese army goes back on a program of modernization, and a very somewhat puzzling figure, certainly a critical player in this process, is a man named Yuan Shikai.

Yuan Shikai we met briefly earlier in the context of the 1898 reforms. He was one of the Chinese officials who turned against the reformers, sided with the Empress Dowager Cixi and took part in the suppression of the reforms in 1898, which in some ways seems out of character. Perhaps as a modernizer, as an advocate of the modern army within the Qing state, one would have expected to see him be on the side of the reforms of 1898, but for his own reasons, he chose not to support them, but instead to ally himself with a conservative elements amongst the Manchu leadership, but that winds up preserving his power and influence; and in the first decade of the 20th century, he's one of the more powerful figures, and certainly one of the more powerful Chinese officials within the Qing government.

In 1911, he comes to play a pivotal role. The modern military, the modern units within the military had become a focal point for political activity. This in some ways was probably an unintended consequence of the efforts to modernize the army, but the officer corps in particular—and especially the junior officers, who were reasonably well educated, were exposed to Western ideas, not just about military affairs but about history and politics—began to develop ideas of their own, which were rather radical and progressive. The Revolutionary League—the Tongmeng hui, Sun Yatsen's organization—devoted a lot of effort to trying to organize among the ranks of the junior officers in the army, and they were reasonably successful in doing this. Many junior officers join the Revolutionary League; many junior officers were involved in conspiratorial groups thinking about planning different kinds of insurrections.

In October of 1911, one of these groups in Wuhan in central China was plotting some bombings, preparing to try to trigger a popular uprising, and their activities were accidentally discovered. A bomb that was being prepared by one of them within a part of the city that was actually under the control of the Russians—it was a Russian economic concession—exploded unintentionally, it wasn't supposed to go off at that time, and as a result of that, the authorities became suspicious and they began to prepare to round up and arrest some of the politically outspoken members of the army. This triggered a defensive move on the part of the radical soldiers, and they launched a coup within Wuhan, and arrested senior officers, arrested some of the local representatives of the Qing government, the local magistrates, and called upon the military and the people to support them in a rebellion against the Qing dynasty.

They proclaimed a Republic in the province in which Wuhan is located, Hubei province, and they proclaimed the independence of that province from the Qing Empire. Over the next few weeks, other military units in other provinces, particularly initially in central China but then spreading to other parts of the empire, followed suit and proclaimed their independence, disavowed their allegiance to the Qing state. These events were largely spontaneous, they were triggered by this accidental uncovering of a plot in Wuhan, but they spread quite quickly and began to be coordinated from one location to another.

Interestingly enough, Sun Yatsen was not even in China at the time that this rebellion breaks out. During what will prove to be the end of the empire and the foundation of the Republic, the great revolutionary leader wasn't even on the scene. He was actually in Denver, Colorado when he received word of the Wuhan rebellion. He was on a speaking tour, raising money to continue his political work. He sets out to return to China. One might think he would go back west to San Francisco and sail immediately across the Pacific, but instead he continues on around the world, east across America, across the Atlantic to Europe, speaks there a bit, and eventually makes his way back to China. He doesn't arrive back in China until the end of December of 1911.

Before he gets back, as he is making his way back and as events are continuing to develop in China, the revolutionary movement begins to realize that they're about to be successful, that the dynasty is in fact on its last legs. They need to figure out what they're going to do about that, how they're going to cope with the disappearance of the Qing state. This is where Yuan Shikai comes back into the story and plays what becomes a very critical and pivotal role. Yuan Shikai was at this point the commander of what's called the Baiyeng Army. Baiyeng means northern ocean, and it just simply refers to the modern military forces that are in northern China. In that capacity, he was located, he was based very close to the capital, and of course he had very good political access to the Manchu elite. What Yuan Shikai does is to position himself as the middleman, as the broker between the revolutionary forces in central and southern China, who are, after all, at this point strongly based within the modern military. So, he has a natural connection to them, and the dynasty, where he also has his political links.

Yuan Shikai is in an ideal position to be the broker, to be the intermediary between the two power centers at this time. What he does is to negotiate on behalf of the nascent republic the abdication of the Qing dynasty. This becomes a very delicate process, and Yuan Shikai is certainly not acting as a neutral and disinterested party. The natural expectation was that when Sun Yatsen returned to China, he would assume the leadership of the republic. He was the leader of the revolutionary movement, everyone recognized and respected him, and there was an expectation or assumption that he would step into the role of the leader of the new government. Indeed, on January 1 of 1912, when the republic is formally proclaimed, Sun Yatsen is named as president. He's going to, he is put in position as the leader of the new regime. But as part of the deal that Yuan Shikai negotiates with the dynasty, Sun has to agree to step down as president when the emperor abdicates and to allow Yuan Shikai to become president. Indeed, this is exactly what happens. The emperor finally abdicates in February of 1912, Sun Yatsen resigns the presidency of the republic, and Yuan Shikai is named to assume that post.

The plan in the winter of 1912 was that Yuan Shikai's presidency was a provisional one. There was no constitution yet. There was no institutional structure for a permanent government of the republic, and the idea was that Yuan Shikai would serve as president during the period when the preparations would be made to establish a more stable and permanent regime. The critical event in this process was the election of a provisional national assembly in the fall of 1912, because it was the duty of that body to then produce a constitution. Accordingly, elections were organized and held, and Sun Yatsen's group, which now was transformed from the Tongmeng hui, the Revolutionary League, to what's called the Guomindang, the National People's Party, or the Nationalist Party, as it's normally referred to. The Guomindang emerged as the clear victor, winning the most seats in the new assembly, and Sun Yatsen was clearly positioned to guide the party forward in the writing of the constitution and probably then in leading the Republic.

However, when the assembly met, when it was going to begin to deliberate the future of the republic, Yuan Shikai was unwilling to allow this process to go forward. Sun Yatsen had been elected but had decided not to take a seat in the provisional assembly. He wanted to preserve his special status. Clearly, he had in mind keeping free to assume the position of president again. Instead, the leader of the Nationalist Party in the provisional assembly was a man named Song Jiaoren. Song Jiaoren, when he was standing on the railway platform in Shanghai, preparing to board the train to go off to take his seat in the assembly, was assassinated, and it was quite evident quite soon that this assassination had been orchestrated by Yuan Shikai to eliminate a strong leader on the part of the Nationalists in the assembly.

That was not sufficient; and indeed, as the assembly began its deliberations, Yuan Shikai was increasingly unhappy with them and eventually dissolves the assembly, expels the Nationalist delegates from the assembly and then allows a rump legislature to meet without the Nationalists, and that legislature approves a constitution, under the terms of which Yuan Shikai was named as president for life. So the idea of establishing a constitutional republic with an elected assembly goes by the boards fairly quickly, and the republic has a rather abortive launch.

Yuan Shikai's career is not yet over, and he in fact remains as president for three more years after 1913, when he dissolves the assembly and has himself made president for life. Indeed, by 1916, by the spring of 1916, Yuan Shikai had conceived the idea that he might establish a new imperial dynasty. He has robes made for himself in the imperial style, he assembles around himself a group of officials suitable to be a Confucian imperial cabinet, and in March of 1916, actually goes out to perform some of the old imperial sacrifices at the temple of heaven in Beijing and attempts to proclaim himself emperor. But this is too much, even for his more loyal followers, and his effort at an imperial restoration with himself as emperor collapses. He flees the capital just a short time after this, and on his way south towards his hometown, in central China, he dies, ostensibly of a broken heart at the frustration of his imperial ambitions.

The death of Yuan Shikai, while in some ways certainly a relief, in some ways could potentially have been seen as removing an obstacle to the establishment of a viable republic, instead proves to be only a further stage in the collapse of political authority in China. Once Yuan Shikai dies, the last really strong, charismatic figure who had provided a sense of national identity, national cohesion and some substantive organizational effectiveness is removed from the scene. What follows is a period of about a decade during which China basically falls apart. Military strongmen emerge in different parts of the country. Some of them had been generals or high-ranking officers in the old imperial army; some of them were individuals who had risen to prominence in the early years of the republic under Yuan Shikai. Others were simply individuals who seized the opportunity now to grab power wherever they could, and warlords, as they come to be called, established control all across China.

There really was, from 1916 until 1926-27, no effective central government in China. There was no single capital, certainly Beijing or Nanjing continue to function from time to time as the seat of governments that claimed to be the national government of China; but in practice, there was no such thing during this period. The warlords fought amongst themselves, sometimes forming alliances. Sometimes those would break up, and former allies would go to war with each other. It was a time of great hardship, great suffering in China. It was a time when the foreign powers continued to enhance their own positions—particularly the Japanese became much more ambitious in their efforts to take over and control parts of China—and it was a time when this process of humiliation and weakness and breakdown that went back all the way to the Opium War really reached its peak. Out of that chaos, and in the context of that chaos, new voices, new ideas about ways to put China on even more radical course of transformation began to be heard. We'll start to listen to those in next lecture.

Lecture Thirty-Two
The New Culture Movement and May 4ᵗʰ

Scope:

Chinese intellectuals and new urban elites completely rejected the traditional imperial system and the Confucian ideology that had been its official orthodoxy. New kinds of ideas were sought that would allow China to regain internal cohesion and develop into a modern country with the kind of power and prestige it had possessed in the past. Nationalism, a belief in science and democracy, anarchism, and other European ideas began to spread, as did the pragmatism of the American thinker John Dewey. At the same time, a profound disillusionment with the practical political actions of the Western powers began to spread. After the Versailles Peace Conference agreed to give Japan control of former German-held territories in China, thousands of students took to the streets of Beijing on May 4, 1919, fighting with the police and burning down the house of the foreign minister. This ferment of ideas and political movements set the stage for the emergence of the Chinese Communist Party.

Outline

I. With the collapse of the last dynasty, many Chinese repudiated the whole imperial tradition.

   A. The Confucian political culture was seen as a dead weight on Chinese society.

      1. Scholars and writers rejected the use of the classical literary language and, instead, advocated *baihua*, the plain vernacular language of daily speech.

      2. The values of Confucian social relations and ritual were seen as rigid impediments to democratic egalitarianism.

      3. Confucianism was seen as oppressing women and young people and privileging the elite over ordinary workers and farmers.

   B. The New Culture Movement sought modern alternatives to the Confucian past.

      1. New magazines and literary journals in plain language were published.

      2. Ideas about science, democracy, and various kinds of European philosophies were discussed.

     3. Western thinkers, such as John Dewey, George Bernard Shaw, and Bertrand Russell, visited China and gave public talks about their ideas.

  C. Other movements were more concerned with organizing workers.

     1. Chinese anarchists began to build unions even before the collapse of the Qing.

     2. In the 1910s, anarchists were the largest mass political movement in China.

     3. Ideas about socialism, feminism, and radical egalitarianism were propagated by the anarchists and by socialists and other Chinese students returning from study in Japan.

II. World War I provided first hope, then frustration for the Chinese.

  A. During the war, Chinese industry was able to make gains.

     1. As the Western powers were concerned with events in Europe, Chinese businessmen took the opportunity to expand their operations and gain market share both at home and abroad.

     2. Hundreds of thousands of Chinese workers went to France to replace French workers who had joined the army.

     3. These workers sent home both money and ideas and brought back their experiences of unions, elections, and radical politics.

  B. At the end of the war, Western promises of "self-determination" proved to be hollow rhetoric.

     1. The Allies had justified the war, in part, as a campaign for the "self-determination of peoples."

     2. At Versailles, however, the victors divided up the spoils of the defeated and made clear their intention to retain their own colonial empires.

     3. In 1915, Japan had delivered to the Chinese government a program, known as "The 21 Demands," aimed at facilitating Japanese domination of China, which the Chinese refused to accept. After the war, Japan, which had formally been on the Allied side, was allowed to keep the former German concessions it had occupied during the war.

    4. China, which had also been an ally and had sent much real aid to France, was forced to agree to the terms of the treaty.

III. The May 4th Movement broke out as a response to the betrayal at Versailles.

    A. When news of the decision in Paris reached China, students took to the streets of Beijing.

        1. Several thousand rallied at Tiananmen, where the government ministries stood.

        2. They marched east toward the Western legations but were blocked by police.

        3. They then burned down the home of the foreign minister.

        4. Several students were arrested and many more were beaten by police.

    B. The movement spread beyond Beijing and was embraced by merchants and workers, as well.

        1. Strikes and boycotts against Japanese businesses and goods took place in many Chinese cities.

        2. Eventually, the government had to release arrested students, and the Chinese delegation at Versailles refused to sign the final version of the treaty.

    C. The May 4th Movement and the New Culture Movement created a basis for the rise of the Chinese Communist Party.

        1. In the wake of the Bolshevik Revolution in Russia in 1917, news about Marxism and Leninism spread in China.

        2. Chinese who had rejected the imperial past and who now felt betrayed by the Western liberal democracies began to turn to communism as a new alternative.

        3. The Chinese Communist Party would come to be the most serious force seeking to transform China. We will follow its early development in the next lecture.

Essential Reading:

Chow Tse-tsung, *The May Fourth Movement*.

Supplemental Reading:

Arif Dirlik, *Anarchism in the Chinese Revolution*.

Questions to Consider:

1. Why was language reform so important to the progressive intellectuals of the early 20th century?

2. Given that both China and Japan had supported the Allies in the First World War, why did the Versailles Peace Conference agree to allow Japan to retain the former German concessions in China?

Lecture Thirty-Two—Transcript
The New Culture Movement and May 4th

The end of the imperial system in China was in part a political process. Of course, the destruction of the Qing dynasty, the elimination of the institutional structure of government was central to the process, but the political culture that had surrounded the Qing state, the imperial state itself was part of what many Chinese came to see as the problem—the dead weight of the past, it was often seen as, which was holding China back from its modernization, from assuming a new role in the modern world. With the collapse of the dynasty, many Chinese embarked upon a pretty thorough repudiation of all aspects of the traditional culture. If they didn't completely reject it, they certainly developed an extremely critical perspective on ideas, institutions, and ways of behaving that had been part and parcel of the old imperial order.

In particular, the Confucian heritage was seen as having been a major component and still constituting a major obstacle in the path of a changing China, of a new China. In the same years that the republic was in a sense being stillborn—when Yuan Shikai was seizing power for himself and then after his death, as China fragmented into a network of warlord power centers, the critique of traditional culture and the beginning of the advocacy of new ideas, new solutions, very radical departures from the way things had been done and thought of in China—this process went on, even while the political system was breaking down further and further. This period in the 1910s, is sometimes referred to as the New Culture Movement, and at the end of the decade, we get what comes to be called the May 4 Movement. I want in this lecture to talk about these two very closely interrelated phenomena, the New Culture Movement and the May 4 Movement.

The New Culture Movement, as its name would suggest, was about making a new cultural system for China and, of course, to embark upon the process of creating something new. Many Chinese also felt it was necessary first to go through a process of criticizing and breaking with what was old. So the rejection of the old culture is really integral to this process of New Culture Movement. Central to this in many instances was the question of language. Chinese elite culture, Chinese political culture in particular, was intimately bound up with the use of the classical Chinese language, the literary Chinese language, which was very different from the way that ordinary Chinese spoke in their day-to-day lives. Classical Chinese was based upon the language as it had existed perhaps 2,000 years earlier, as it had been preserved in the writings of Confucius and Mencius and the other sages of antiquity, and they had remained very true to those origins and had, in fact, become increasingly alienated from the ordinary speech of people as the centuries passed on.

Now, educated Chinese began to advocate the use of what we call *baihua*, meaning simple language, plain language. Writing Chinese as it was spoken, using in essence a vernacular Chinese, just day-to-day common Chinese when they wrote about, not just the portrayal perhaps of conversations in fiction, where more simple speech had been used for while, but even in articles, essays talking about the great political issues of the day, talking about reform in government and history and art and literature. The use of baihua, the vernacular language, comes to be a marker, a sign of who's modern and who's not. Those who continue to use the classical language were seen as anachronistic, were seen as throwbacks to a former time, and the people who wanted to be perceived as progressive, as part of the new China, of forging the path to the future, wrote in a much more simple and accessible kind of language.

This classical language, of course, had embedded within it the values of Confucianism, the ideas about hierarchical social relations, relationships of mutual obligation. These are now seen as essentially having been oppressive. The reciprocal aspect of Confucian relationships, which we talked about quite a while ago, was lost, was largely eclipsed by a focus on the idea of all social relationships being hierarchical, and the sense of the superiority of the ruler or the husband or the father was now seen as dictatorial and as oppressive and needing to be rejected and repudiated, and a more egalitarian set of social relationships and ideals needing to be adopted.

In particular, Confucianism came to be seen as bound up with the specific oppression of many groups within society. Women, peasants, workers all were seen as having been disadvantaged, as having been seen as little people, lesser people, as opposed to the position of men or of the educated elite, who were seen as having been validated and valorized by the ideals of Confucianism. Confucian ideology, Confucian ideas, terms, cultural practices, all come to be seen by progressive Chinese as part of the problem, and as things that need to be done away with and overcome. This rejection of Confucian culture, this turning away from the Confucian past, goes along in tandem with a search for new ideas, for new ways to address the concerns of the day.

This search was carried out largely in the pages of a lot of journals that came to be circulated at this time. One in particular, called *New Youth*, was very important. It became a forum for debate on a wide range of ideas. Many of these ideas, not surprisingly, came from the West, were drawn from Western thinkers, from the countries, from the cultures which were seen by the Chinese as being the most successful, as being the dominant groups, exerting their power over China because of the strength, because of the superiority of their cultural systems at home. Western thinkers became very popular figures in China at this time. Quite a few of them traveled to China, went on speaking tours to express their ideas to try to encourage educated young Chinese to modernize themselves, to adopt the ideas of these Western teachers. Figures like John Dewey, George Bernard Shaw, Bertrand Russell all went on these kinds of speaking tours in China late in the 1910s or in the early 1920s.

Other groups emerged within Chinese society during these years as well, with perhaps a less sophisticated set of concerns and programs, but which were also very influential in spreading new ideas and new ways of coping with the challenges of life in the modern world. In particular, interestingly, anarchists were very active in China. Anarchism at the end of the 19th and beginning of the 20th century in the West was a significant political movement. Anarchist groups in European countries like France and Italy, and perhaps most significantly Spain, were not simply isolated bomb throwers, but were large organizations of workers, often deeply embedded in trade union movements; and it was in this context that we can see the spread of anarchist ideas to China. Anarchism became a significant political force in Japan about this time, and overseas students, Chinese students who were studying outside of China, some in Japan and another group interestingly in Paris, in France, became very interested in the ideas of anarchists and began to write about these, publish journals about these and ship these back to China.

Indeed, anarchists founded the first unions, the first organized groups of workers in China, even before the fall of the Qing dynasty. Actually, barbers in southern China were the first Chinese workers to be organized, and they were part of this anarchist movement. The anarchists spread ideas which were a rather diverse. They talked about socialism, they talked about feminism, they had very radical egalitarian ideas, and before long, other groups, which were more devoted to these particular aspects of political thought—feminist groups, socialist groups—began to appear in China as well. During the 1910s, during this period of the New Culture Movement, while intellectuals, members of the educated elite were debating the repudiation of Confucianism and the more genteel ideas of Shaw and Russell and Dewey, the anarchists were working to build mass movements, workers' organizations to try to create the conditions for a socialist transformation in China as well.

World War I, of course, is taking place while all this is going on. World War I, from 1914 to 1918, becomes a period which in some ways is very beneficial for China, becomes a period of opportunity for China, but in other ways can also see some new problems, some new adverse circumstances arise for China. On the one hand, economically, the period of the First World War was an opportunity for China. European industry was, of course, largely diverted to wartime production, and this allowed certain Chinese industrial sectors to expand their role in the market, particularly in the textile industry, but in a few other sectors as well. The Japanese, in fact, owned many of the factories in China, which were able to take advantage of this; this is also a period where the Japanese do rather well. Some Chinese businessmen who own their own factories were also able to take advantage of this business opportunity during the First World War, and so there's a mini-boom for the business community in China during these years.

At the same time, hundreds of thousands of Chinese workers traveled to Europe, particularly to France, where they took jobs in factories, many of which had been abandoned by young men who had gone off to military service. These workers, Chinese workers in France, became a very significant force because on the one hand, they sent home money. They earned money and they sent a large proportion of what they earned to their families back in China. So this again was a positive economic influence that took place. Perhaps more significant in the long term, by being exposed to European, French trade unions, to the conditions in European factories, to the ideas of democracy, education, liberty, equality, fraternity, those hallmarks of French political rhetoric, they also began to transmit those influences back to China, and these ideas were not merely the province of well educated intellectuals, but increasingly were in circulation in ordinary society as well.

The end of the First World War proves to be a critical time; and here we have to take a minute and think about the relationship between China and Japan. China, as we've already talked about, back at the end of the 19th century in 1894 to 1895, had fought a war with Japan, in which it had been soundly defeated. The Japanese have launched themselves on their program of national recreation, if you will, in the middle of the 19th century and had achieved great success in this by the 1890s. As they moved into the 20th century, their successes continued. In 1904-1905, they fought a war with the Russians and defeated them. This was a remarkable event for an Asian country to defeat the European power, even if it was Russia, which was the weak link in the European system. Nonetheless, it was significant that a yellow nation had defeated a white nation. This was seen as quite dramatic at the time.

The Japanese had gone on to annex Korea, to make it part of the empire. They had already gained the island of Taiwan from China as a result of the settlement back in 1895. The Japanese empire was expanding, and the Japanese were increasingly turning their perspective, conceiving their ambitions in terms of the Asian mainland. When World War I comes along, the Japanese see a window of opportunity. There are of course a number of opportunities for the Japanese at this time, but their situation in China is one of great concern to them. The European powers, which while certainly wishing in their own ways to dominate and exploit the situation in China, have recognized that China is an area where all the powers played on an equal level. The Americans in particular had been very clear since John Hay's "Open Door Notes" back at the beginning of the 20th century that there should be no special spheres of influence in China, that all the ports should be open to all the powers, an equal opportunity approach to Western imperialism.

But during World War I, the Japanese had a special opportunity because the Western powers were clearly focused on what was happening in Europe. They weren't able to devote as much attention to the situation in China. Accordingly, in 1915, the Japanese delivered to the Chinese government—and at that time Yuan Shikai was still president and there was still a single government entity to address—they delivered to the Chinese government what are called the 21 Demands. The 21 Demands are essentially a program to facilitate Japanese domination in China. They won a special economic concession; they wanted the ability to place Japanese officials as overseers in Chinese government offices. Basically, they were demanding to be given a unique special status which would allow them to dominate and control much of public life and economic life in China.

The Chinese government doesn't accept the 21 Demands; they don't agree to the concessions which Japan is seeking, but this pressure that the Japanese put on China was quite severe, and it was quite intimidating to the Chinese. When World War I had broken out, the Japanese declared themselves as belligerents on the side of the Allies. Of course, they were far away from Europe and in some ways this was not a particularly significant move, but the Germans had possessions, territorial possessions in China and in the Western Pacific. They had, of course, the port of Qingdao that we've mentioned earlier, and Shandong province and a few other concessions on the Chinese mainland, and they possessed a number of islands in the Western Pacific, which they had been developing as a source for various minerals and other resources. The Japanese occupied these German concessions. They sent military forces and simply took over these concessions and held them for the duration of the war.

In 1919, when the war was over, the great peace conference was convened at Versailles in France. It was at the Versailles negotiations that things went from bad to worse for the Chinese. The Chinese had of course also been Allies, they had been part of the Western alliance of the British and the French and the Americans against Germany and the Austro-Hungarian Empire, but while the Japanese were rewarded for their support, the Chinese wound up being essentially left in the lurch. Of course, there's a great irony and frustration involved in this. The Western powers during World War I had, of course, proclaimed it as a war to make the world safe for democracy. The American president Wilson in his Fourteen Points had proclaimed that among the war's aims was the idea of self-determination for peoples. Not surprisingly, many people around the world, particularly in colonial countries, countries that were colonies of the European powers, interpreted the idea of self-determination for people's as meaning that after the war, after they had supported their colonial masters, after they had sent troops off to fight and die in the war, that they would then be allowed a greater role in self determination, that they might even attain independence and self rule.

It became very clear at the Versailles peace conference that the Western powers had no intention whatsoever of allowing the colonial peoples self-determination; that in fact, the maintenance of the colonial order was at the top of the agenda for the Western powers. In particular for China, this was made clear when the former German territorial concessions in China, rather than being returned to Chinese control at the end of the war, were granted to Japan. Japan had seized them militarily at the beginning of the war, and now was given the right to retain them. This was seen as a real betrayal by the Chinese, and when word of this reached Beijing, a telegram arrives in Beijing, it sparked demonstrations which became the focal point then of what we come to call the May 4 Movement.

The word came overnight from Paris on May 3 that these were the terms of the treaty that China was being presented with, and students gathered the next day at noon at Tiananmen, the great gate at the southern entrance to the imperial city, where the government ministries were located. This area today has been expanded into the great square, the great public space and Tiananmen Square. Several thousand, many thousands of students assembled at Tiananmen midday on May 4, 1919, and they marched eastward along the main east-west street there in Beijing towards the Western diplomatic quarter. The police blocked their access to the diplomatic quarter, so they turned aside into the narrow alleyways off of to the north, where they went to the home of the foreign minister. The Chinese foreign minister in the cabinet at that point was seen as having been weak, as having betrayed China by allowing the Chinese delegation at Versailles to be part of these negotiations. In fact, the Chinese government never accepts the terms of the treaty, but the treaty is imposed anyway, even without their signature, their authorization for it.

When they reach the home of the foreign minister, they burn it down. They enter the home first and beat up a gentleman they find there who they thought was the foreign minister. It turned out, in fact, he wasn't; the foreign minister had put on the dress of a female servant and fled out the back door. The crowd was so enraged they went ahead then and burned down the house. Police arrived, there were confrontations between the students and the police. Several students were rested, others were beaten, and the demonstration eventually is broken up.

Political tension in the capital persists over the following days. Officials from Beijing University get involved, officials from the government in Beijing, which is only one of the many centers of warlord power but is still presenting itself as the national government at this time, they get involved. Eventually, students are released, the students make demands on the government about not ratifying the treaty, and the government has to accede to that. The movement spreads far beyond the capital. It spreads to many other cities around China, and it spreads beyond the ranks of students. In fact, it becomes a very popular movement. Many merchants join in the movement, in part because one of the tactics that the movement adopts is a boycott against Japanese goods. Obviously, if you're boycotting Japanese goods, you're going to be buying Chinese goods, or at least somebody else's goods, hopefully Chinese goods, and so many Chinese businessmen support the May 4 Movement as well.

The May 4 Movement—we talk about the May 4 demonstration, the actual events of May 4 1919—the May 4 Movement in a sense merges, flows into what's going on with the New Culture Movement as part of this process of criticizing the past, seeking new ideas, new ways to address China's problems. What's most important about the May 4 Movement is the idea that it represents a loss of face for the West and a loss of faith in the West on the part of many educated young Chinese. The hopes, the aspirations for a liberal democratic republican kind of system, which had been around in China since the struggle to overthrow the Qing dynasty, have now run up against the realities of the pragmatic interests of the Western powers, and the betrayal as it's perceived in China of the ideas of self-determination, of making the world safe for democracy, the war aims of the Western powers are now perceived by many as having been duplicitous, as having been lies, and that the Chinese are now once again victimized and humiliated by the Western powers, even as they have been trying to emulate the Western way.

In conjunction with these events, other developments outside China have also been taking place, and word of these begins to weave into this process of political discussion and debate that's going on with the New Culture Movement and the May 4 Movement. Of course, what I'm referring to here is the Bolshevik Revolution. The Bolshevik Revolution beginning in October of 1917, in Russia, has tremendous impact in China. Word of it doesn't arrive immediately, and really it's not until the spring of 1918 that many Chinese begin to have a very clear idea of what's going on next door in Russia. But there are a number of aspects of the situation in Russia that have a very dramatic impact on the thinking of educated and more radical Chinese. For one thing, the Czarist state was the closest in some ways parallel in Europe to the situation of China. The Czar had the same sorts of powers that the old Chinese emperors had. The Russian empire was a vast expanse, not unlike China, a large peasant—in many ways pre-industrial—society; and yet, here there had been this revolutionary upsurge. And when the Bolsheviks proclaimed their new order, proclaimed socialism, socialist democracy, denounced the secret diplomacy of the Western powers, all this was very well received by progressive Chinese.

The discussions of alternative paths to the future in China now began to turn more and more to an examination of the ideas associated with the Bolshevik Revolution, the ideas of Marxism, the ideas of Leninism, the Communist strategy, the idea of a Communist party as a revolutionary organization which could lead China into the future. The establishment of the Chinese Communist Party would follow quite closely on these events, and we will pick up that story in the next lecture.

Lecture Thirty-Three
The Chinese Communists, 1921–1937

Scope:

The Chinese Communist Party (CCP) was founded in Shanghai in 1921. It grew out of discussion groups in Beijing and elsewhere and with the help of advisors from the Soviet Union. In the early 1920s, the Communists and the Nationalists, led by Sun Yatsen, formed an alliance, but after Sun's death in 1925, this collapsed as the new Nationalist leader, Chiang Kaishek, sought to destroy the CCP. In 1927, Chiang launched all-out attacks on Communists and drove the Party out of China's cities. In response, largely influenced by the ideas of Mao Zedong, the Party turned to a peasant strategy, relying on agricultural workers to build the revolution. After a period of experimentation in the early 1930s and following the epic Long March from southeast to northwest China, the CCP established its main base area in Shaanxi province in 1936 and, in 1937, managed to form a new alliance with the Nationalists.

Outline

I. The Chinese Communist Party was founded in Shanghai in 1921 and soon sought an alliance with the Nationalists.

   A. The Party was established through the actions of Chinese Marxists and Soviet advisors.

   1. Study groups in Beijing and other cities had been meeting since 1919.

   2. Advisors sent by the Communist International in Moscow worked with Chinese Marxists, including Li Dazhao and Chen Duxiu.

   3. The First Party Congress was held in July–August 1921 in Shanghai, with a handful of delegates in attendance.

   B. Realizing that they did not have the strength to lead a revolution right away, the members of the CCP sought an alliance with the Nationalist Guomindang (GMD).

   1. The GMD was still led by Sun Yatsen, who had been impressed with the organizational efficiency of the Bolshevik Party.

    2. Sun was willing to work with the CCP as long as Communists accepted the leading role of the Nationalists.

    3. The First United Front allowed Communists to join the GMD as individuals, and many, such as Mao Zedong, rose to positions of responsibility and influence.

II. In 1925, Sun Yatsen died, and the CCP-GMD alliance began to crumble.

  A. Sun was succeeded as leader of the GMD by Chiang Kaishek.

    1. Chiang was a military man who had been leader of the GMD military academy at Whampoa, near Guangzhou.

    2. He had studied in the Soviet Union and formed a strong aversion to the Communists.

    3. After Sun's death, Chiang was one of several strong leaders in the GMD.

    4. He used his control of the army to intimidate and outflank his rivals and eventually became supreme leader.

  B. In 1926, Chiang launched the Northern Expedition to reunite China.

    1. The GMD had been in control only of Guangdong province in the far south.

    2. Chiang led GMD forces north and either defeated or bribed local warlords, bringing them into the GMD regime.

    3. In April 1927, he reached Shanghai but allowed local gangsters and secret GMD agents to wipe out the Communists in the city before bringing his army in to take control.

    4. This precipitated a split with the CCP, and a major purge of Communists in all GMD-controlled cities followed.

III. The CCP had to find a new way to survive.

  A. For a while, urban Communists and their Soviet advisors tried to carry on as before.

    1. The main Party leadership called for uprisings and strikes, but these actions were all failures.

2. Leadership in the Party changed hands repeatedly.

B. In the countryside, a new strategy was evolving, largely led by Mao Zedong.
1. Mao had been director of the GMD's Peasant Bureau.
2. He believed that "agricultural workers" could be the main force in the revolution.
3. A rural base area was set up in southern Jiangxi, where Communist policies could be tried out and refined, including early efforts at land reform.

C. Chiang Kaishek completed the unification of China and turned his attention to the eradication of the Communists.
1. By the end of the 1920s, the northern warlords had been brought under GMD control, and a new national government was installed in Nanjing.
2. Chiang saw the CCP as his main enemy, despite Japanese aggression in Manchuria, which was seized in September 1931.
3. In the early 1930s, Chiang launched repeated campaigns to destroy the CCP bases in Jiangxi.

IV. The Communists embarked on the Long March to reach northwest China and build a new base of operations.

A. In the autumn of 1934, it became apparent that Chiang was preparing a final assault on the CCP's base.
1. Communist leaders decided to abandon the Jiangxi Soviet and go to northwest China, where another small base area already existed.
2. In October 1934, 115,000 people set out on foot, leaving a small contingent behind to make a last stand against the GMD.
3. Over the next year, the CCP forces walked across much of southwest and northwest China, crossing mountains, marshes, deep gorges, and barren deserts, reaching Shaanxi province late in 1935.
4. Of the 115,000 who set out on the Long March, only about 15,000 survived, and they became heroes of the revolution, respected even today for the sacrifices they made.

B. Once in their new base in Yenan, Mao and the CCP leaders turned to resisting Japanese aggression and to building their movement for a New China, even forming a Second United Front with the GMD in December 1936. We will follow that story in the next lecture.

Essential Reading:

Lucien Bianco, *Origins of the Chinese Revolution, 1915–1949.*

Supplemental Reading:

Harrison Salisbury, *The Long March.*

Edgar Snow, *Red Star over China.*

Questions to Consider:

1. Why was Chiang Kaishek so obsessed with the Chinese Communists and so willing to ignore the expansionist ambitions of Japan?

2. How could Mao Zedong justify his advocacy of a leading role for peasants in the revolution, given the Marxist ideology of the working class as the main force in modern history?

Lecture Thirty-Three—Transcript
The Chinese Communists, 1921–1937

The end of the second decade of the 20th century, China had gone through ten years of post-imperial turmoil. The First World War had come and gone, and the hopes of perhaps an improved situation in the world after the war had been dashed by the Versailles peace conference. Many Chinese had begun to search for radical alternatives to the ideas that had brought China to its present circumstances, whether those were the traditional Confucian political culture or the more liberal democratic ideas associated with the hopes of the republican movement. At the beginning of the 1920s, a new ideology, which had grown out of the activities of the anarchists and socialists earlier in the century, and particularly from the influence of the Bolshevik Revolution in 1917, took root in China and took on institutional form in the founding of the Chinese Communist Party.

The Party was founded in Shanghai in 1921. It was the result, the get-together in July that actually put the Party institutionally in place, formally in place, was the result of a process that had been going on for couple of years. Marxist study groups in Beijing and Shanghai and other places had sprung up in the wake of the First World War and the Bolshevik Revolution. These had grown in size, they had begun to reach out and try to form links to workers' organizations, to socialist groups in other parts of the country. Beginning around 1920, as the Soviet Union began to pull itself together, and the Communist International, the Third International was established; agents sent out from Moscow began to visit various parts of Asia and China, in particular, to assist in the process of revolutionary organization. In China, agents from the Communist International were involved both with the establishment of the Chinese Communist Party and with the reorganization of Sun Yatsen's Nationalist Party. We'll talk about the Nationalists in a minute, but first I want to finish with getting the Communists organized.

These advisers from the International who came to China worked with the Marxist study groups, began to do the groundwork to establish a national organization, and they helped to suggest the terms of a program, the organizational format for the new party, and in the summer of 1921, assisted with the convening of the First Party Congress. There were only about a dozen delegates at the First Party

Congress. Many people were unable to travel to Shanghai to attend. Some of the people who were among this first dozen drifted off into relative obscurity afterwards. One individual who was present—although not because he had been all that important an actor up to this point, but certainly would become so later—was Mao Zedong. Mao Zedong from Hunan province in central China had been living in Beijing, had been exposed to the Marxist study groups there through his work at the library in Beijing, and had made his way to Shanghai and was able to take part in this initial gathering.

The Communist advisers to both the new party and to the Nationalists put forward an analysis of the situation in China, which called for an alliance, a united front between the Communists and the Nationalists. The Nationalist Party, which was still under the leadership of Sun Yatsen in the early 1920s, was reorganized internally, along the disciplined lines of the Bolshevik Party, of the Russian Communist Party, and this made the Nationalist Party a much more effective organization than it had previously been. One of the problems, one of the frustrations that Sun Yatsen had faced in his life was that he was a good orator, he was a good speaker, a good fund raiser, a good propagandist, but he wasn't much of an organizer, and he didn't seem to have figured out a way to make the Nationalist Party into a truly effective political force.

The advice of the Communists, and the organizational changes that they helped to put in place within the Nationalist Party, gave it greater cohesion, greater internal discipline, and turned it into a more functional political organization. This did not mean that the Nationalist Party or Sun Yatsen embraced the Marxist-Leninist ideology of the Bolsheviks or of the advisers from the International, but it did mean that Sun Yatsen in particular was more open to some kind of cooperation, some sort of collaboration between the new Communist Party and his Nationalist Party.

The First United Front was accordingly put together, and under the terms of this, individual members of the Chinese Communist Party could join the Nationalist Party, could be members in other words of both parties, and could indeed even serve as officers within units of the Nationalist Party. The Communist Party was not to join the Nationalist Party organizationally; in other words, there wasn't a merger between the two parties, but individuals can be members of both parties. Many individual Communists did join the Nationalist

Party, participated within political activities of the Nationalist Party, and some even rose to positions of relative prominence within the Nationalist Party, including—with great significance for later developments—Mao Zedong, who became leader of the Peasant Bureau within the Nationalist Party. The peasantry was, of course, not seen as the most important group; urban workers, industrial proletariat were seen as the focal points by both the Nationalists and the Communists. So Mao's position in dealing with the peasantry was not a particularly prestigious one, but it becomes his experience there, and the ideas that he developed there become quite important, as we shall see later on.

In 1925, Sun Yatsen dies, and this is a critical turning point, because so long as Sun Yatsen was alive, so long as he was dedicated to his particular vision of the Nationalist revolution and of a socially progressive version of nationalism, the alliance with the Communist Party made a lot of sense. The Communist Party was still relatively small, it certainly wasn't an organizational threat to the Nationalists early on, and Sun's willingness to work together resulted in benefits for both sides. It allowed the Communist Party grow and gain a lot of experience, but it also benefited the Nationalist Party. Much of the work the Communist organizers did was quite diligent and quite effective, and they actually brought a lot of members into the Nationalist Party, non-Communist members into the Nationalist Party.

In the wake of Sun Yatsen's death, something of a leadership vacuum develops at the top of the Nationalist Party and it takes a little while, a year or so, for a successor figure, a single successor figure to really emerge. When that happens, the individual who comes to dominate the Nationalist Party, first as a military leader and eventually as its political leader as well is Chiang Kaishek. Chiang Kaishek himself is a very interesting figure. He was a military man, and he had been sent by Sun Yatsen to study in Russia and to learn about the Bolshevik Revolution, to learn about the Communist systems of organization, to learn about the Red Army, and he had spent six months studying and working in Russia. When he came back from that experience, he was very impressed with the organizational skills and techniques of the Bolsheviks, but he was a confirmed anti-Communist. He was very opposed to the political program of the Russian revolution and the Communist Party.

Chiang Kaishek became the commandant of the Nationalist military academy at Whampoa outside of Canton—Guangzhou in Guangdong province—and in that position was able to establish quite a network of personal connections and loyalties within the Nationalist military. He used his influence within the army, and his position as leader of the Nationalist Army, as a factor in the political maneuvering that took place after Sun Yatsen's death, and used that as a way to advance his own position and eventually to emerge as the new strongman within the Nationalist Party. In 1926, the year after Sun Yatsen's death, Chiang Kaishek finally felt himself to be in a strong enough position within the Nationalist movement, and felt the Nationalist movement itself to be strong enough militarily to launch an effort to re-unify China.

What he undertakes we call the Northern Expedition. The Nationalists had their base down south in Guangdong province. Guangdong province had essentially been the only part of China that the Nationalist Party could control. The rest of China had, of course, been divided up amongst the various warlords, and it's in some ways possible to see Chiang Kaishek as simply one of these warlords who happened to have the Nationalist Party as his political machine. Be that as it may, the Northern Expedition, when it gets underway in 1926, proves to be a very successful undertaking. The Nationalist armies essentially follow the same route that the Taiping movement had followed back in the 1850s, moving from Guangdong province up through central China, through Hunan to the Yangzi River valley and then turning east and heading towards Nanjing, and moving a little more quickly than the Taipings had.

Over the course simply of a few months, they managed to gain control of most of southern China. This happens through a variety of mechanisms. In some instances, the Nationalist forces fight against the forces of local warlords, and they generally win. They defeat the local leaders and absorb them then into the Nationalist forces. In other instances, Chiang Kaishek was able to negotiate political arrangements, under which the local warlords would pledge their loyalty to him and would therefore be brought under the Nationalist umbrella. In other instances, he simply bribed people. He would buy the loyalty of individuals who couldn't be appealed to on any other basis and who he didn't feel like fighting or didn't wish to risk fighting. By one means or another, the Northern Expedition succeeds, by the spring of 1927, in basically getting all of southern China south of the Yangzi River into Nationalist hands.

In April of 1927, the Nationalist forces have reached the outskirts of Shanghai. At this point, Chiang Kaishek makes a decision that is of great political significance. He has reluctantly up to this point maintained the United Front with the Communist Party which Sun Yatsen had put in place. Not wishing to jeopardize his own position as the heir of Sun Yatsen, as the successor of Sun Yatsen, he hasn't felt until now strong enough to do anything other than continue his policy. But by April of 1927, having successfully carried out the Northern Expedition, having gained all this control over half of China, he feels his position to be much stronger, and so he decides to do away with the Communists, to eliminate them not just as partners in the United Front, but to try to drive them out, to try to destroy them as a political force in China.

Accordingly, when the Nationalist forces reach the outskirts of Shanghai, he stops, he does not take the Nationalist army into the city, but instead allows Communist organizers within the city and within the trade unions in the city—Shanghai was by this time the most industrialized city in China; within factories there were many thousands and thousands of workers, most of whom were organized into trade unions with at least links to, if not being dominated by the Communist Party—when the Nationalist army is approaching Shanghai, the Communists launch an uprising. The idea being to seize the city from within so that the Nationalist army won't have to fight its way in, but Chiang Kaishek stops outside of Shanghai and doesn't intervene, doesn't come in; and the insurrection in Shanghai is then suppressed by a combination of the troops of the foreign powers—Shanghai is an international city, so the British, the French, the Americans, the Germans at this time, the Japanese rather, all have forces there—and those forces, those police and military units are mobilized to attack the workers, to attack the Communists; and in conjunction with those government forces of the foreign powers, the secret societies, the organized crime circles within Shanghai also come out and start to attack the workers and the Communist organizers.

This combination of the foreign powers and the Shanghai underworld destroy the Communist movement in Shanghai. Many hundreds of Communist organizers and leaders are arrested and executed. Others die in fighting in the streets. Many workers are shot or arrested and imprisoned, and some of them executed, even if they weren't members of the Communist Party. It's a very bloody uprising and suppression of the Communist movement in Shanghai; and it represents, it signals the break, the split between the Nationalist Party and the Communist Party.

It takes a while for this political process to completely unfold. A left-wing group within the Nationalist Party, which is centered at the city of Wuhan on the central Yangzi River, continues to ally itself with the Communist Party for a while; but before long, Chiang Kaishek is able to convince them that they really need to split with the Communists and stick with him. He intimidates them militarily, and by the end of the summer of 1927, the left wing of the Nationalist Party reunites with Chiang Kaishek's mainstream, and Chiang now is the disputed leader of the Nationalist movement and of a Nationalist movement, which is no longer—in his view—hampered by this alliance with the Chinese Communist Party.

The Chinese Communist Party finds itself in a difficult situation. Their principal political orientation up to this time had been towards organizing urban workers. The classical theories of Marxism had emphasized the role of the industrial working class as the vanguard of the revolution. This was the force which would lead the transformation of society, build socialism. But now the organizational base of the Chinese Communist Party in the cities, amongst the industrial workers, is destroyed. Shanghai was the most important location, but once this rupture takes place in Shanghai, it's repeated elsewhere, in other ports, in other centers of industry, and the Communists are systematically driven out of urban China. How is the Party to survive? What are they to do?

It's at this point that the role of Mao Zedong begins to be significant. Mao Zedong, as leader of the Peasant Bureau of the Nationalist Party, had spent a lot of time in the countryside, had spent a lot of time observing what was happening away from the cities, away from the great coastal ports in places like his home province of Hunan. What he saw was large peasant movements, not unlike peasant movements that we've seen in earlier times in Chinese history, but now movements which were taking place in the modern world, in a modern context, and which could be imbued with a modern ideology and led by—in Mao's view—a modern political party. He saw the uprisings of the peasants as a very powerful force, a force so powerful, that, as he put it to his comrades, their choice was to either try to lead it, or just to get out of the way, because this movement was going to sweep across the country; and if the Communist Party could lead it, they could turn it into a revolutionary force.

These ideas had been pretty marginal up until this time, but in the wake of the suppression of the Party in the cities, Mao's ideas suddenly began to seem a little more reasonable. This doesn't happen overnight; in fact, it takes a number of years for Mao's ideas to begin to be accepted and to begin to be dominant within the Chinese Communist Party. Initially, when the Party is devastated in the cities, the remnants of the Party leadership and the advisers from the Soviet Union simply call for greater revolution, and they urge Communists in various parts of the country to launch insurrections and to try to jumpstart the revolution, and this leads to a series of really disastrous uprisings. Mao himself is drawn into one of these when he is ordered to lead a peasant army to capture a city in central China. They do so for a few days, but then they're driven out by the better armed and better organized forces of the Nationalist army, and it's after this that Mao retreats with the remnants of his peasant army to the mountains of southern Jiangxi province, is there, along with other local Communist leaders and the remnants of a few others of these abortive uprisings, that he begins to put together a new model for the Chinese Communist movement.

This rural base area, as it comes to be called, in essence becomes a laboratory; and in the early 1930s, Mao and a man named Zhu De, who was a Communist military leader, and Zhou Enlai, who became one of Mao's greatest political allies, these individuals work together with several million peasants in southern Jiangxi to create a Communist experiment, to carry out experiments in land reform, in reforming the Chinese family system, a variety of things which later on, after the Communist Party comes to power nationally, will be implemented in a fully developed way. But in the early '30s, in Jiangxi, they're just experimenting; they're trying things out in a laboratory of peasant society. Chiang Kaishek went on after 1927, to complete the unification of China. In 1928, he takes his forces on to the north, defeats or wins over the remaining warlords, and establishes a re-unified China, a single Nationalist government now based at Nanjing again, with Chiang Kaishek as the leader, comes to be put in place.

Even while he's completing the second half of the Northern Expedition, Chiang begins to have conflicts with the Japanese. Japanese military units are in Shandong province to protect their concession at Qingdao and some of their railway lines. There are confrontations between Japanese military units and Chiang's forces in 1928, in Shandong. Later on, the Japanese blow up the train of one of Chiang's warlord allies in northern China because they want to eliminate him as a threat to their position in Korea. Tensions between Chiang Kaishek and the Japanese, between China and the Japanese begin to show a little more clearly at the end of the 1920s and beginning of the 1930s, but Chiang Kaishek determines that the real problem that he needs to deal with, the real enemy that he faces is not the Japanese, but the Chinese. He says very famously that the Japanese are disease of the skin, where the Communists are a disease of the guts. He's willing to ignore the activities of the Japanese to a great extent and concentrates his efforts on fighting against the Communists.

The base area in southern Jiangxi—which is only one of a number of these areas where local Communist forces establish control, but it's probably the most significant one—becomes the focal point of Chiang's activities in the early 1930s. He launches a series of what are called "encirclement campaigns," where he basically puts a blockade of military forces completely surrounding the Communist base area and then slowly but surely closing the ring, moving closer and closer in. The first several of these efforts are defeated. The Communists manage to fight back and drive off the Nationalist forces, but Chiang keeps the pressure up. He begins in the 30s to get military advice from the Germans. The Nazi Party that has come to power in Germany in the early '30s, begins to form a fairly close working relationship with Chiang that will be suspended later when they become even more closely allied with the Japanese, but for a while in the mid-30s, German advisers are very helpful in leading the anti-Communist campaigns for Chiang Kaishek.

Eventually, by 1934, it becomes apparent that the latest encirclement campaign of the Nationalists against the Jiangxi base area—which is sometimes called the Jiangxi-Soviet—is going to be successful, and the Communist leaders then have to decide what they're going to do, how they're going to cope with this threat. What they decide to leads to one of the most dramatic events in 20th century Chinese history, an event which continues to inspire young Chinese even today. This is what's called the Long March. In October of 1934, the Communists decide that they're not going to be able to resist Chiang Kaishek and the encirclement campaign much longer. There is another base area far away in northwestern China, centered on a small town called Yenan, and they decide that they're going to try to break out from the Jiangxi area and make their way to Yenan. This is a long way to go, and they don't know exactly how to get there or how they will survive in the process of doing so.

Nonetheless, they figure this is their best option, their only real chance. In mid-October 1934, 115,000 people break out from the encirclement, a small contingent is left behind in the heartland of the Jiangxi base area to make a last stand against the Nationalist forces, and also to keep those Nationalist forces occupied so that they won't be able to pursue the Long Marchers as they set out. The Long March strikes off to the south and west, and in the course of the next year, they troop over several thousand kilometers. It's not a simple straight path off to the northwest that they take. They travel through several provinces, they have to cross mountain ranges, swamps, deep river gorges, it's a very dramatic event, they're constantly being pursued and harassed by Nationalist forces. Of the 115,000 people who embark on the Long March, 15,000 complete it; so 100,000 people are lost one way or another along the way.

Early in the course of the Long March, a very important political event takes place, which is that Mao Zedong is named leader of the Communist movement. He assumes the position of Chairman of the Party, and he holds this position uninterruptedly until his death in 1976. The triumph of Mao sets the stage for the latter part of the Chinese revolution. Once the Long March reaches Yenan at the end of 1935, the great age of what comes to be called the Yenan era or the Yenan base era get started; and in the northwest, the Communists have a new laboratory, a new arena in which to experiment with their policies and organizational methods. Later on, when the Japanese invasion comes, the Yenan base area will be the center of resistance against the Japanese invasion; and indeed, by the end of 1936, from their position in the northwest, they're able to enter into a Second United Front with the Nationalists. We'll see the circumstances of that, and how the war with Japan and the revolution which follows it play out, in our next lecture.

Lecture Thirty-Four
War and Revolution

Scope:

The Second United Front was not really effective, but it did last in some form throughout the war against Japan. Once Japan was defeated, though, civil war followed quickly. Despite massive aid from the United States, the Nationalists were defeated by the Chinese Red Army in 1949, and Chiang's forces withdrew to the island of Taiwan. The Chinese Communists, under Mao's leadership, set about creating a "New China" and launched a program of building socialism. Land reform, a new marriage law, and the nationalization of urban industry were the first steps. The Korean War threatened to disrupt this process, but China managed to prevent an American invasion and to pursue its new policies with aid from the Soviet Union in the 1950s.

Outline

I. In December 1936, the CCP and GMD formed a new United Front.

   A. GMD General Zhang Xueliang "arrested" Chiang Kaishek and forced him to negotiate with the Communists.
   1. The "Xian Incident," named for the city near which it took place, reflected the frustration of many patriotic Chinese with Chiang's refusal to fight the Japanese.
   2. The CCP agreed to join in a new alliance to resist Japan's aggression in northeast China.
   3. Chiang accepted the agreement, but Zhang Xueliang was kept under arrest until the 1990s.

   B. The Second United Front lasted through World War II, but was never fully effective.
   1. Japan launched a full-scale invasion of China in July 1937.
   2. The GMD was forced to retreat to Chongqing, in Sichuan, while Japan occupied much of northern and central China.
   3. Japanese atrocities at Nanjing—what came to be known as the Rape of Nanjing— and elsewhere stiffened Chinese resistance.

    4. The CCP led a guerrilla war against the Japanese from bases in Shaanxi.

II. By 1944, Japan's defeat was seen as inevitable, and both the GMD and CCP began to prepare for the postwar period.

  A. Chiang hoarded military supplies from the United States in preparation for attacking the CCP once the war with Japan was over.

    1. Frustration with Chiang's attitude led to clashes with his American military advisor, Joseph Stilwell.

    2. Chiang knew that the Americans would defeat Japan and didn't want to expend his forces fighting the occupation army.

  B. The CCP saw the coming end of the war as the chance to extend the revolutionary struggle.

    1. Communist activism against the Japanese had greatly expanded support for the revolution among the farmers of north China.

    2. The CCP saw Chiang as hopelessly corrupt.

  C. When Japan surrendered, there was a period of negotiation, but civil war broke out before long.

    1. The United States sent negotiators to try to keep the peace in China, but by the middle of 1946, the confrontation between the CCP and the GMD was beyond control.

    2. The United States aided Chiang's forces and turned over supplies from the defeated Japanese to them.

    3. The Russians gave the CCP some aid from their occupation of Manchuria.

    4. Major fighting took place through 1948, and by early 1949, it was clear that the CCP would win.

III. The People's Republic of China (PRC) was established in 1949.

  A. The Nationalists withdrew to Taiwan.

    1. The Battle of Huai-Hai in November 1948 signaled the end for Chiang's army.

    2. He ordered the withdrawal to Taiwan, after first carrying out a massacre of Taiwanese dissidents.

  B. On October 1, 1949, Mao Zedong proclaimed the establishment of the PRC in Beijing.

1. The new government set about stabilizing China, then launched a program of Socialist transformation.
2. The foundation of the program was land reform, in which the economic back of the old literati elite was finally broken.
3. The government also passed a new marriage law, which gave women freedom to marry whom they pleased and to own property.
4. Urban industry began to be nationalized, and the financial system was brought under government control.

C. An alliance with the Soviet Union brought material aid to China, but the Korean War threatened the new regime.
1. Mao signed a treaty of friendship with Moscow in 1950.
2. Soviet advisors came to China in great numbers to help with building projects and educational reform.
3. The civil war in Korea threatened to bring American troops into northeast China, but massive Chinese intervention saved the North Koreans and protected China's frontier.
4. The stage was set for the pursuit of Mao's image of a "New China"; we will examine the major steps in that process in the next lecture.

Essential Reading:

Jonathan Spence, *Mao Zedong*.

Supplemental Reading:

John Fitzgerald, *Awakening China*.

Chalmers Johnson, *Peasant Nationalism and Communist Power*.

Questions to Consider:

1. The Communist Party led the most active resistance to the Japanese occupation, and won widespread support among the peasantry of northern China. Was this a sufficient basis for carrying out its revolutionary program?

2. Chiang Kaishek relied on the United States to win the war with Japan. Did he then expect that the United States would intervene in China's civil war?

Lecture Thirty-Four—Transcript
War and Revolution

At the end of 1935, Mao Zedong and the 15,000 survivors of the Long March arrived in northwestern China. They spent much of 1936, settling into their new circumstances in the Yenan base area; and at the end of that year, an opportunity arose for the establishment of a Second United Front between Communists and Nationalists, with a focus at this point on resisting the Japanese. The occasion that allows for the formation of the Second United Front is something that's called the "Xian Incident." Xian is the modern name for the ancient city that had been Chang'an in Shaanxi province, and at that time in 1936, this part of China, the southern part of Shaanxi province, was in the control of one of the military strongmen who was part of the Nationalist coalition, part of the Nationalist alliance.

This was a man named Zhang Xueliang. Zhang Xueliang's father had been a warlord in northern China, and he had been assassinated by the Japanese back in 1928, so Zhang Xueliang was particularly anxious that China and the Nationalists should take a strong stand against Japanese aggression, and he was very frustrated with what he perceived as Chiang Kaishek's unwillingness to stand up to the Japanese. Chiang, as we've noted before, saw the Japanese threat as secondary and the threat of the Communists as primary, but Zhang Xueliang saw it the other way around, and he was anxious to encourage Chiang Kaishek to take a stronger line of resisting the Japanese.

What happens in the Xian Incident is that Chiang Kaishek goes to Xian to visit Zhang Xueliang, and during that visit; General Zhang effectively places Chiang Kaishek under house arrest. He then invites representatives from the Communist base area in northern Shaanxi province to come to Xian and the Communists send Zhou Enlai, and he enters into negotiations, and an agreement is reached for the forming of a united front to resist the Japanese. Chiang Kaishek is released and goes back to Nanjing, to his capital, but he then places Zhang Xueliang under arrest; and in fact. General Zhang remains under arrest by the Nationalist forces right down until the end of the 1990s. He was taken to Taiwan when the Nationalists fled in 1948-49, and was held under house arrest there until just about 5-6 years ago.

Nonetheless, the terms of the united front brought the Communists and the Nationalist forces together to strengthen China's ability to resist Japan. As it turned out, the timing on this was very significant. In 1931, Japan had invaded Manchuria and had occupied that part of China, had actually separated it from China and created a puppet state called Manchuguo, with the last of the Manchus emperors, Puyi, now as the ruler, the puppet ruler of this supposedly independent country. In July of 1937, Japan launched a full-scale invasion of China proper. There's a famous incident in July of 1937: the so-called Marco Polo Bridge Incident takes place at a site southwest of Beijing, where Chinese and Japanese troops have a confrontation, and from that, the war breaks out steadily through the rest of 1937.

The Japanese, once they launch their invasion of China proper, pursue it quite vigorously, quite relentlessly along two basic lines. They come into China from the north, crossing the Great Wall from their puppet state in Manchuria, and start to move south along basically along the railway lines running from Beijing down to central China to the central Chinese city of Wuhan. That's a north-to-south advance, which doesn't go very rapidly, but that's the line that they wanted to follow. The second front that they open up starts with the city of Shanghai. Shanghai was, as we've mentioned before, an international city. There were British, French, Americans, Russians and Japanese and others living in Shanghai, and many of the foreign countries that were represented there had their own troop concentrations, their own military units there. In the fall of 1937, Japanese forces based in Shanghai attack the Chinese part of the city, the western side of Shanghai, and then begin to fight their way west up the course of the Yangzi River.

The Japanese plan was that the group moving west up the Yangzi River and the group moving south down the railway from the Beijing would meet at the central Chinese city of Wuhan, and they expected this to happen fairly quickly. The idea was to have almost a blitzkrieg, a lightning sort of invasion, but that did not work out. In fact, both in north China—and especially along the Yangzi River—the resistance that the Chinese put up was much more intense, much more fierce than the Japanese had anticipated. In some ways, this should recall the experience that both the Mongols and the Manchus had in invading China, where the greatest resistance that they met was in the Jiangnan region. They were coming into the region from the north and the west, whereas the Japanese were invading from the east and coming out of the city of Shanghai, but in either case, the Jiangnan region proved to be a very difficult area for a foreign conqueror to move through.

Nonetheless, the Japanese were able to eventually achieve their initial military objectives, and the Nationalist government was forced to retreat first from the city of Nanjing, west up the river to Wuhan, and then eventually forced to abandon Wuhan and move on up through the Yangzi Gorges to the city of Chongqing in Sichuan province, where they established what proved to be their permanent wartime headquarters. When the Japanese reached Nanjing, which had been the Nationalist capital, it took them until December, the beginning of December of 1937, to actually get there. When they did—again in recollection or certainly in residence with the events of the Manchu conquest—the Japanese carried out at Nanjing a great massacre. They were very upset, they were very frustrated with the resistance that the Chinese had put up, and when they took the city of Nanjing, although the Chinese military had largely withdrawn, the Japanese unleashed a very serious campaign of terror against the civilian population of Nanjing.

Hundreds of thousands of people were killed, many women were raped, and the incident comes to be known as the Rape of Nanjing, and is still today a source of very severe tensions sometimes between China and Japan. The atrocities that were perpetrated there and elsewhere in China, while they were certainly intended by the Japanese to terrorize and intimidate the Chinese, often had exactly the opposite effect—certainly of frightening people, but had the opposite of the intended effect, which was to make the Chinese stiffen in their resistance, to make them even stronger in their hostility to the Japanese invasion. Once the Japanese had managed to occupy particularly northern China, the war after the first year or two begins to settle into a more stable pattern. The Nationalists were based in the west and the southwest. They had their political center at Chongqing in Sichuan province, and another very important center down at Kunming, in Yunnan.

They also had troops still in various parts of south China. The Japanese do not occupy all of south China by any means, and so there were pockets, there were areas where Nationalist forces continue to operate long after the initial Japanese invasion. In the north, the Chinese Communists had their base area in Shaanxi province around the town of Yenan, and from there the Communists pursued a campaign, a very vigorous campaign of guerilla warfare all across north China. The idea that the Japanese were occupying all of north China was a little simplistic. During the daytime, they could extend their presence over many areas; but at night, except for the areas right along the main railway lines and in the main towns, much of the countryside was in the hands of popular forces led by Communist guerrillas. So, there was lots of sabotage, lots of fighting, ambushing of Japanese troops, blowing up of bridges and railway lines and things like that, designed to harass and tie down large numbers of Japanese troops who could not be spared then for other kinds of military uses.

This pattern then persisted for several years, with the Japanese occupying much of China, not really being able to push their conquests to further, not being able to really gain complete functional control even of the areas that they basically were dominating militarily. Their invasion of China, which theoretically was designed to help them solve their problems at home, their economic and population problems in Japan proper, it proved to be a very counterproductive activity. But once they had invaded, once they had occupied China, the Japanese really had from their point of view no choice but to try to stick things out and hope to eventually defeat their enemies in the war and perhaps reap some benefits of victory down the way. That clearly was not the direction that the war took; and by 1944, it was pretty clear that Japan's defeat was inevitable. The war in the larger Pacific theater, the war with the United States, was one which, after the first few months, it became evident Japan could not win, despite the dramatic victories that they achieved at the end of 1941 and beginning of 1942. By the summer of 1944, the American counterattack was moving relentlessly towards Japan, and it became obvious that the USA would defeat Japanese imperialism, and that would radically transform the situation in China.

In anticipation of eventual American victory, Chiang Kaishek and the Nationalists pursued a relatively static strategy vis-à-vis the Japanese. They resisted Japanese attempts to acquire more territory, but they didn't really launch major offensives to drive the Japanese out of territory they already occupied. Chiang Kaishek received a lot of military assistance from the United States during the war, and he tended to store that away, to save it for the postwar period, where he anticipated a great conflict with the Chinese Communists. Frustration with this on the part of the Western Allies, particularly American military adviser Joseph Stillwell, resulted in tensions and almost an open break between Stillwell and Chiang. Eventually, Stillwell had to be withdrawn by the American government, but Chiang stayed resolute in his view that, even after Japan had invaded and occupied so much of China, they were not the real problem and that the real enemy was going to be the Chinese Communist party.

As for themselves, the Party, the Chinese Communists saw the coming end of the war as setting the stage for a great revolutionary confrontation between their popular movement, their peasant-based movement, and the Nationalist government. The anti-Japanese resistance, which Communist guerrillas had spearheaded, particularly across northern China, had won them widespread support. The Communists were certainly perceived at least as having been the more active fighters in the resistance against Japan, and this helped to spread, along with some fairly modest programs of social reform that the Communist pursued in their areas under the patrol, this led to a great deepening of popular support for the Red Army and for the Chinese Communist movement in general. Meanwhile, the Communists were able to present an image of the Nationalists and of Chiang Kaishek as corrupt, as unpatriotic, as incompetent, and as basically being the agents of Western imperialist interests in China. The split, the division between the Communists and the Nationalists, even though there was theoretically this united front to resist the Japanese, the antagonism between two parties certainly did not diminish and probably only intensified in the course of the war.

When Japan surrendered in September of 1945, there was a period in China where efforts were made to try and negotiate some sort of postwar perhaps coalition government. The United States sent negotiators 2-3 times to China to bring leaders of the Nationalist and Communist movements together, but while that was going on, there was a lot of maneuvering taking place on the ground. The Russians had come into the war at the very last minute, in August of 1945, just shortly before the atomic bombs were dropped on Japan, but in doing so, they had come into northeast China, into Manchuria, and occupied a lot of the territory that had formerly been in Japanese hands. They stripped a lot of the industrial plant from that area and took it back to the Soviet Union as war reparations, but they also passed some aid along to the Chinese Communist forces. The United States at the same time was turning over large amounts of Japanese arms that had been captured after the Japanese forces in China surrendered to the Nationalists. So, although negotiations to try and find some sort of peaceful coalition were going on, both sides, both the Communist and the Nationalists, were also strengthening their positions militarily, preparing for a real serious confrontation.

When these efforts to negotiate some sort of compromise solution broke down—which didn't take all that long, certainly by the end of 1946—full-scale fighting breaks out between the Communists and the Nationalist. The Nationalists first drive the CCP out of their base area in the northwest, but that proves to be a relatively meaningless victory because it's in the North China Plain, the great heartland of peasant farmland, that the Communists now have their greatest strength and up in Manchuria. So, northern China, Manchuria and the North China Plain, falls fairly quickly under the control of the Communists. Southern China and the southwest tend to remain in the hands of the Nationalists initially, and then a great military confrontation between these two areas follows.

In 1948, late in 1948, a great battle takes place called the battle of the Huai-Hai. The Huai River runs through central China between the Yellow River in the north, and the Yangzi River to the south; and on the plains surrounding the Huai River, a great battle takes place, a great tank battle, one of the few really large conventional warfare set-piece battles that we have in the Chinese revolution. The Communist forces emerge victorious. They defeat the Nationalists. The Nationalist military is deeply demoralized by this time. Communist propaganda is being increasingly effective in presenting the Communists as the wave of the future, the true Nationalists in some ways, the true patriots, and the corruption, the inflation that's taking place in the zone under Nationalist control is making the lives of ordinary Chinese increasingly difficult, and so it's not surprising that political support for the Nationalists disintegrates, and the military situation deteriorates for them as well.

After the Nationalist defeat in November of '48, in the Huai-Hai battle, Chiang Kaishek begins to withdraw his forces to the island of Taiwan, which will become his last outpost. There are still large Nationalist forces spread across southern China at this time, and most of those will eventually be withdrawn over to Taiwan. Some

Nationalist forces in the far southwest wind up going across the border into Burma, and many of their descendants remain there even today. The withdrawal to Taiwan is preceded, late in 1948, by an uprising of the indigenous Taiwanese population, who are not too happy about the idea of their island being taken over by the Nationalist forces from the mainland; but Chiang Kaishek carries out—Nationalist forces carry out—a fairly large-scale massacre of dissidents and resisters in Taiwan, and pacify the island to prepare it for the Nationalist withdrawal. The state of martial law which is imposed on Taiwan at that point late in 1948 stays in effect for over 40 years.

Nineteen forty-nine is the great year of transition. This is the year when Nationalist forces are driven further south, isolated in various parts of the country, and are either allowed to surrender or are annihilated; and Chiang's forces eventually begin their withdrawal across the straits of Taiwan to the offshore islands. In April of 1949, Communist forces enter Beijing. The city had been besieged since the fall of 1948, but through careful negotiations, it is surrendered to the Communist forces without a major battle, without major destruction of the cultural heritage of the capital, and that's something that certainly Beijing people and others were very grateful for. Over the summer of 1949, as Communist forces advanced everywhere across China, the leadership settled in Beijing and began to prepare the establishment of a new government.

On October 1 of 1949, that new government, the People's Republic of China, is proclaimed by Mao Zedong in a speech at Tiananmen, the Gate of Heavenly Peace, the former southern entry to the imperial palace complex; and he at that point issues his very famous statement that the Chinese people have stood up, and the establishment of the People's Republic is portrayed—certainly by the Chinese leadership—as finally achieving the goals that had led to the overthrow of the old imperial regime back in 1911-1912—had been frustrated with the failure of the Republic initially, had been threatened even more by the fragmentation of China under warlordism, and then through the Japanese invasion and the civil war with the Nationalists. Finally, here in October of 1949, Mao is saying this is over, the long period of warfare and division and oppression by foreigners and reactionary forces in China is over.

The People's Republic of China allows the Chinese people to take control of their own destiny. A very dramatic moment, a very dramatic speech by Mao, and not entirely out of line with the realities of the situation, which were in that, for the first time in a very long time, there was a single, unified, national government in China with a coherent and disciplined and basically honest, not corrupt institutional core in the Chinese Communist Party, and the Communists were set upon a program which in their view would end China's weaknesses and would begin the process of building what they consistently quite hopefully called a "New China."

The core of their program was land reform. They had already begun the process of land reform, even before the formal proclamation of the People's Republic. Indeed, we talked in the previous lecture about the Jiangxi Soviet back in the early 1930s and how the Communists had experimented with various social policies there. One of the things they had tried out there was how to go about land reform, how to redistribute land to make sure that you didn't have some people who owned large estates, others who had no land at all and perhaps could only sell their labor as tenants or day workers. How could you achieve a more equitable distribution of land? As a still predominantly agricultural society, land was the most important productive resource. So land reform becomes the core of the new program.

Beginning in 1948, and continuing into the early 1950s, the new regime, the Communist Party and the government of People's Republic, oversaw a fairly comprehensive program of land reform: first in the areas in north China, which they had occupied and controlled pretty consistently since the end of the Second World War; and then extending this into the newly conquered areas, the newly controlled areas in south and southwestern China. The process of land reform was a very complex one, and the Communists were very careful not to simply impose a new structure, a new system on the vast population of rural China. Instead, what they set out to do was to act almost as facilitators in a process. They would send work teams into villages, and they would seek out the people in the villages who had grievances, who seemed the most politically motivated, and they would work with them to identify who the landowners were and what the power relationships within a particular village were; and over a period of weeks, or sometimes months, they would prepare for a moment when they would have mass meetings and assemble the farmers and have them denounce the landlords and seize the estates or seize the deeds, the titles to the land.

Many landlords were beaten; many others were killed in this process. It was a violent transformation of the agricultural system of ownership. It was a very traumatic event, in many instances a very brutal offense, and yet it was the critical event to allow China to break with the economic realities, which had begun to stagnate all the way back in the 18th century, and really hadn't been transformed or hadn't been modernized in any significant way up to the middle of the 20th century. The land reform that was carried out by the Communists, as we will see, doesn't really achieve the objectives of socialism and communism that they had intended; but it does create the material conditions for the establishment of new modes of production, and eventually for the emergence of China as a dynamic and powerful growth economy at the end of the 20th century. We'll return to some of those linkages in the next couple of lectures. Land reform was critical to eliminating the political control of the old rural elites and to creating the conditions of rewarding the peasants for their support of the Party, and to creating the conditions for improving agricultural production.

It was carried out in tandem with other reforms that were directed also at transforming the traditional rural Confucian popular culture; and the most critical step here was the passage of what's called the "Marriage Law." The Marriage Law was meant to abolish certain traditional practices, principally arranged marriage. It allowed people to marry at their own will. It allowed for divorce, it allowed both men and women to initiate divorce; and perhaps most significantly, when the land reform was carried out under the terms of the Marriage Law, land as it was redistributed was not simply given to the head of a household—which would mean that it was basically redistributed among men—but was given to both men and women so that men and women, husband and wife, would each have their own economic resources. This was meant to empower women so that the legal empowerments of divorce and free marriage had some economic support, had some substance to them. These were very radical reforms directed at transforming the core values, the core structures of the traditional system, and they were very effective in doing so. They didn't necessarily achieve the intended outcomes that the Communists had, but they were critical to the ability of China to develop in the future.

The Chinese established an alliance with the Soviet Union, which, as we'll see in the next lecture, was very import for economic development in the course of the 1950s. Soviet advisers came to China, helping with economic development. The war in Korea between the north and the south threatened to bring American troops into China again, but massive Chinese intervention in the fall of 1950, while prolonging the fighting on the peninsula, did keep the Chinese homeland basically secure. By the end of 1950, Communists were certainly in firm control of all of China. They were embarking on their program of socialist construction, and we will follow the course of that construction through the first quarter century of Communist rule in the next lecture.

Lecture Thirty-Five
China under Mao

Scope:

For a quarter of a century, Mao Zedong was the dominant figure in the People's Republic of China, but his prominence should not mask the underlying tensions and disagreements in the Chinese Communist Party. A series of clashes among Party leaders was reflected in the history of the Great Leap Forward, the Socialist Education Movement, and finally, the Great Proletarian Cultural Revolution. This lecture will tease out the complex interaction of differing groups within the Communist leadership and consider how the economic and political development of China fared through Mao's death in 1976.

Outline

I. From 1949 until his death in 1976, Mao Zedong was the dominant figure in China.

   A. Mao's vision of a New China was the avowed goal of the government of the People's Republic.

      1. Within the leadership of the CCP, however, there were divergent views of how to pursue the goals of Socialist development.

      2. Debates and disagreements within the Party shaped the history of the PRC and sometimes broke out into public conflicts.

      3. Mao generally was able to win the day but, at times, had to compromise or give up some of his power to gain his objectives.

   B. In the 1950s, the main area of contention was over agricultural policy.

      1. Following land reform, there was a gradual process of collectivization, which at first, was voluntary and modest in scale.

      2. These early steps were quite successful, and yields rose rapidly, leading to enthusiasm for further collectivization.

3. By 1956, Mao began to urge an accelerated program, which soon led to the creation of the People's Communes, large-scale units of collective farming.
4. The Great Leap Forward in 1958 and 1959 was an attempt to mobilize peasant labor to achieve a "take off" in production that could also provide investment for urban industrial growth.
5. It failed because of bureaucratic over-reporting and exaggerated claims, which triggered excessive consumption and, ultimately, led to food shortages.

II. The failure of the Great Leap led to the first serious clash within the Party.

    A. Through the 1950s, the CCP had carried out political campaigns against "rightists" and "anti-Party elements."

        1. These campaigns were often used by Party bureaucrats to strike at those who criticized their abuses of public trust.

        2. The Party's popularity suffered somewhat from this, but the overall achievements of the revolution still won wide support.

    B. With the Great Leap came the first open clash between Party leaders.

        1. At a conference of top Party leaders in August 1959, the defense minister, Peng Dehuai, criticized Mao.

        2. Mao counterattacked and was able to have Peng removed from office but had to agree to give up control over the day-to-day management of government affairs.

    C. Over the next three years, the CCP adopted more moderate tactics, and a "pragmatist" group, led by Liu Shaoqi and Deng Xiaoping, came to have great influence.

        1. These leaders emphasized the achievement of concrete economic objectives rather than the integration of politics and the economy.

        2. They moved away from the more highly collectivized aspects of Mao's policies.

III. By 1962, Mao began to reassert his leadership.

    A. In 1962, he advocated a Socialist Education Campaign to give Party leaders a better sense of life among the people.

1. Leaders were to "go down" and experience the realities of village and factory life.
2. But senior and mid-level Party leaders didn't want to give up their privileged lifestyles, and the campaign was diverted into another "anti-rightist" episode.

B. Mao became increasingly frustrated and sought to go outside the Party to appeal to the people directly.
1. In 1966, the Great Proletarian Cultural Revolution was launched by Mao without the support of other Party leaders.
2. He called on "the masses" to criticize those in the Party taking "the capitalist road" and behaving like a new ruling elite.
3. The forces unleashed by these actions proved to be more than Mao had anticipated, and after two years of widespread conflict, he began to try to regain Party control.
4. At the Ninth Congress of the CCP in April 1969, the Cultural Revolution was basically ended, though it was carried on in name until Mao's death.

IV. In the years from 1969 to 1976, there was an effective stalemate within the CCP; neither the pragmatists nor the radicals could gain total control.

A. The radical forces were centered in the Gang of Four, with Mao's wife, Jiang Qing, as leader.
1. The Gang of Four controlled much of the information and cultural affairs of the country.
2. In 1971, Mao's designated successor, Lin Biao, was denounced as a traitor and accused of having plotted to kill Mao.

B. The pragmatists, led by Deng Xiaoping since Liu Shaoqi's death in 1969, were purged from power, in theory, but still controlled much of the technical and bureaucratic aspects of the Party and government.
1. Deng had been sent to labor reform in the late 1960s but, by 1972, was in charge of China's science and technology policy.
2. Mao seemed to balance the radicals and pragmatists against one another and was unable or unwilling to give full support to either side.

C. In 1976, a series of dramatic events signaled the coming of a great change.
   1. In January, China's much-loved prime minister, Zhou Enlai, died.
   2. In April, large-scale demonstrations against the Gang of Four took place in Tiananmen Square.
   3. In July, a major earthquake killed nearly 300,000 people in Tangshan, northeast of the capital.
   4. Finally, on September 9, Mao died.
   5. From 1976 on, China had to come to grips with life without Mao, and the post-Mao era soon proved to be one of profound change and dramatic developments.
   6. In the final lecture, we will consider China after Mao and prospects for China and the world at the dawn of the 21st century.

Essential Reading:

Maurice Meisner, *Mao's China and After*.

Supplemental Reading:

William Hinton, *Fanshen: A Documentary of Revolution in a Chinese Village*.

Hong Yong Lee, *The Politics of the Chinese Cultural Revolution*.

Questions to Consider:

1. Why were land reform and the marriage law the first priorities for the new government in 1949–1950?

2. Mao believed that the Communist Party was becoming too bureaucratic and alienated from the masses and that it would become a new elite, replacing the old literati. Was he right?

Lecture Thirty-Five—Transcript
China Under Mao

From 1949 to 1976, Mao Zedong was the leader of the new China. This was a period during which many of the ideals, the visions that he had for building a modern socialist China, went a long way towards being achieved. But it was also a period during which there was conflict within the leadership of the new China over exactly how a modern industrialized society could be built. These disputes eventually brought the party close to self-destruction; and by the time Mao died in 1976, China was poised on the brink of a further radical transformation. What I want to do in this lecture is to consider China under Mao, look at the high points of developments under his leadership, and see how the splits between different groups within the leadership affected the ways in which China evolved and developed during this quarter century.

Mao Zedong's vision of a new China was the dominant rhetoric throughout this period. What Mao said—his writings, his speeches—these were the public goals. These were the ideals that the Chinese Communist Party and the People's Republic of China officially pursued. But almost from the beginning of the People's Republic, there were different groups within the leadership who interpreted the goals of building socialism and building a modern industrial society in different ways, who saw different roads, different paths, if you will, that could be followed in pursuit of these objectives. These debates were generally kept within the leadership of the Party. The Party sought to present—as long as possible—a unified public face, but we know now, particularly in retrospect, that many of these divisions became quite acrimonious, and on occasion they broke out into more public forms of conflict.

Mao was generally able to prevail—at least in terms of keeping the Party line, the stated positions of the Party in accord with his views—but from time to time, he was forced to compromise, sometimes to give up some of his control over various aspects of the government, and he never really was able to have the kind of absolute power over all aspects of development, all aspects of the program of the Party or the government which he probably would have wished, and which would have allowed him perhaps to pursue his particular vision more successfully.

In the 1950s, the principal area of contention between different groupings within the Party had to do with agricultural policy. China at this time was still overwhelmingly an agricultural nation; the agricultural sector within the economy was far the largest, and nearly 80 percent of the Chinese people still lived on the land and were still involved in farming, so how to deal with the agricultural sector was a critical question. Land reform, which we talked about in the last lecture, was carried out across the country and was very effective in redistributing land, getting land into the hands of farming families so that basically all the peasants, all the farmers across China, had some land. Everybody wound up with something. They had individual titles to this land, they could cultivate it themselves; and the great estates, the great landlords, were largely done away with, either given smaller plots of land to farm themselves, or in many instances driven off the land or sometimes killed, and a completely new set up in the countryside seemed to be taking shape.

The goal of land reform and the goal of the Communist movement was not simply to redistribute land to small-scale peasant farmers and have them then go on with a system of small-scale private property, but was instead to build up a collective system, a system of collective or cooperative farming, which would allow various kinds of economic reforms to take place, and which would allow for economies of scale to be developed, and would increase the productivity of the land. In the early and mid-'50s, incremental steps were taken towards agricultural collectivization. It's a very long and elaborate process, and we'll go through all the individual steps of it, but essentially from a widespread body of individual farmers to small-scale cooperative units, to larger-scale cooperatives, and then eventually to be even larger scale collective units. This was a year-by-year process of development.

Up until about 1956 or 1957, each stage in this process seemed to be very effective. There was very little popular resistance or resentment to this, largely because the kinds of reforms that were being carried out, the introduction of some small-scale mechanization, the introduction of better knowledge about techniques of cultivation, the use of fertilizers, cooperation between working groups, the ability to share certain instruments of production, whether it was livestock or farm tools of one kind or another, all these factors combined to result in increasing yields; and if you look at the statistics on food production, grain production in China during this period, year to year they go steadily up. Indeed, grain production increases at a rate faster than population growth, which itself is taking place significantly during these years, and that means that the available food supply per capita was also increasing. So, the reforms that have been carried out in the early and mid-'50s, were very effective and were very successful, and therefore were well received.

By about 1957, Mao becomes convinced that it's possible, building on these initial successes, to accelerate the timeline, to shorten the amount of time needed to achieve complete collectivization. He begins to announce that now is the time to move to the highest level, to what come to be called the People's Communes, which were very large collective entities. He says that communes are a good thing, and a movement effectively sweeps across the country to leap up to these highest level cooperatives, collectives, and to then launch what comes to be called the Great Leap Forward. The Great Leap Forward is in some ways the logical culmination of Mao's vision of unleashing the productive capacity of the Chinese peasantry, of moving to economies of scale, great large-scale cooperative labor projects, to build water reservoirs and irrigation systems.

The Great Leap achieves many very positive objectives, but it runs into some even more powerful negative forces. The core problem that develops with the Great Leap Forward is linked in many ways to Mao's idea of how to motivate people, how to get the vast masses of China to work together and achieve—almost by an act of will—the process of economic development. Enthusiasm is basic in this process, and the enthusiasm for success is such that people begin to falsify their reports of success, not in a gross way, not in an excessive way, but if you add a few percentage points at the bottom level of reporting, and the person at the next level adds a few percentage points, and the person at the next level adds a few percentage points, by the time we get to the national level, the level where the state council, the state planning bureau is formulating its information, making its plans for the future, you have gross distortions in what's going on. That's exactly what happens in 1957, 1958, 1959.

Initially, the Great Leap Forward itself is a huge success. Crop production increases. The problem is it doesn't increase in reality as much as it increases on paper. It does gain, but it doesn't gain as much. Based on false figures, based on misunderstood realities in the

©2004 The Teaching Company.

countryside, the planners decide so much has been achieved, they can lift various kinds of rationing restrictions, they can allow people to basically consume what they want. This results in a lot of grain, a lot of livestock, a lot of food resources of one kind and another not making their way into the supply system for the cities, where they're at the same time trying to build up industry and raise the standard of living in the urban population. Instead, there's initially a glut in the countryside. As a result of that, and as a result of excessively high targets set for the next year, there begins to be a crisis in agricultural production. There's not enough food; food, which they thought was going to be there as a reserve, has been consumed.

As we move into 1959, the situation begins to be much worse. Bad weather sets in, a variety of other circumstances begin to contribute to problems in the countryside, and by the early 1959, food shortages become characteristic. There's a lot of debate, a lot of disputes in academia about the extent of the hunger, the extent of starvation that follows. You'll see figures ranging up to 20 million people dying as a result of the food crisis during the Great Leap Forward. It's hard to know exactly what the precise figure should be, but certainly no matter how you look at it, it's a period of hardship; it's a period of widespread malnutrition and certainly of significant deaths resulting from the shortfalls of the Great Leap Forward.

The crisis that the Great Leap Forward engenders results in the first real serious split, the first real serious division between elements within the Party leadership. There had been campaigns carried out in the course of the '50s, directed against people who were called rightists, or anti-Party elements. These were largely directed against intellectuals who had criticized the Party for being overly bureaucratic. This begins to point up what will prove to be a very serious problem for the Party long-term, which is that it goes from being— prior to 1949—a fighting revolutionary organization, to a government bureaucracy, an administrative elite managing the affairs of the country, and with the capacity to draw to itself a lot of the material rewards and benefits that are being made available by economic growth and development.

The bureaucratic alienation of the Party from ordinary people, from the people which it supposedly is there to serve, starts to be more and more of a problem, and the false reporting of figures during the Great Leap is in one way an example of this, that the bureaucrats wanted to make themselves look good, they wanted to have the best sounding reports, and they weren't really cognizant of how this would have such an adverse impact on the actual lives of the people that they were managing. Needless to say, the food shortfalls that are occurring by the spring of 1959, lead some members of the leadership to be very critical of the policies of the Great Leap Forward. In August of 1959, a party conference takes place, and at that conference, in a place called Lushan, the defense minister at that time a man named Peng Dehuai circulates a letter amongst the Party leadership very critical of Mao Zedong and critical of Mao's model of mass mobilization and modernization based on the agricultural sector and building up the enthusiasm of the peasantry.

Mao learns of this letter and launches a counterattack against Peng Dehuai and eventually confronts the Party leadership with a choice: that if they support Peng Dehuai he will resign, he says, and go back to the countryside and lead a new peasant revolution. Nobody really wants that to happen. Peng Dehuai is forced to resign as Minister of Defense. He goes into an enforced retirement for a few years, although eventually he's brought back to a more active role. But Mao, although he's vindicated, although his leadership is sustained, nonetheless is forced to step back. He's forced to resign from the position of president of the People's Republic, and to retreat to a second stage level in terms of state affairs. He remains chairman of the Party, and of course, wields tremendous power from that position, but it does represent a political compromise that inhibits Mao's ability to manage the operations of the state machinery on a day-to-day basis.

From 1959 until 1962, that state machinery comes to be controlled more and more by a group within the party leadership sometimes referred to as the pragmatists and led by Deng Xiaoping and the president, the man who replaces Mao as president, a man named Liu Shaoqi. These leaders emphasize the achievement of economic objectives, which were thought to be more based on realistic appraisal of things and not on the primacy of politics. Mao's view was that politics should be in command; the more pragmatic wing took the line that economic factors, economic calculations should be given the more significant role. They moved away from Mao's emphasis on the highest levels of collectivization, the People's Communes were largely disassembled and broken back down into much smaller-scale—although still collective—farming entities, and there was a general relaxation in the party's oversight over life both in the countryside and in the cities.

By 1962, Mao began to feel a certain frustration with all of this and with the way things were going, and he wanted to make another effort to remind people of the necessity to keep socialism and the political revolution in mind, as well as the efforts to achieve economic development. He advocated organizing something called the Socialist Education Campaign. The idea of the Socialist Education Campaign was not to educate the people in socialism, but to remind the leadership of how building socialism was in the interest of the masses of the Chinese. The idea was that Party leaders would go down into the villages and would have some direct experience of what life in the countryside, life out in the fields of agricultural production was really like, also in factories in the cities. But senior and even mid-level Party leaders didn't really want to do this. They didn't want to give up the privileges and comforts of their bureaucratic lifestyle; and so, once again, the Socialist Education Campaign winds up being turned into another anti-rightist campaign, and all the old usual suspects, the intellectuals, the critics of the party are once again trotted out and criticized and abused for their supposedly anti-Party or counterrevolutionary sentiments.

Mao found this to be extremely frustrating. He had meant to reform and reinvigorate the Party leadership, and instead the Party leadership had taken this as an occasion to further alienate themselves from elements within the larger population. In 1965, Mao's frustration reaches a peak. He finds that at that point, he has trouble getting some things that he's written published in the newspaper of the Communist Party. This for him is almost unthinkable. He leaves the capital, leaves Beijing, goes down to Shanghai, where there's a group of supporters that share his views and his thinking, and he prepares to launch what comes to be called the Great Proletarian Cultural Revolution. This gets fully underway in the spring of 1966, and over the next 2-3 years engulfs China in a tremendous public drama and public trauma.

What Mao does in the Cultural Revolution, essentially, is to call upon the broad masses to criticize the Party. He says that it is important; he talks about attacking the headquarters. He says that it is right to struggle against reactionaries, and by reactionaries he means people in the Party who are reactionaries. He talks about opposing those in the Party taking what he calls the "capitalist road," whose policies in his view will result in not in the building of socialism, but in China returning to the capitalist way. By calling on the masses, the vast numbers of the Chinese people to attack the Party, Mao unleashes some very powerful forces. We see late in 1966, and into the first half of 1967, some very radical activity. The workers in great cities—most particularly the city of Shanghai, the most industrialized city in China, the greatest port in China, where millions of factory workers lived and worked, but other big industrial cities as well—large-scale mass organizations of workers are formed. Street demonstrations demanding various kinds of reforms take place.

In some ways, what Mao unleashes, the kinds of popular movements that spring up, particularly in places like Shanghai, are almost anticipatory of things like the Solidarity movement in Poland a decade or so later. In Shanghai, in the winter of 1966-67, this actually reaches the point where these popular workers' organizations set aside the leadership of the Communist Party. The Communist Party Committee of Shanghai, the municipal party organization is dissolved, and something called the Shanghai Commune is put in place in February of 1967. But it doesn't last very long, and in many ways this is really the turning point in the Cultural Revolution—it goes on for a while after this, but these events become quite important—because what Mao decides is that you do really need to have a Communist Party. He orders the radical groups in Shanghai to restore the party, to dissolve their popular governments, their so-called Shanghai Commune.

Once he does this, the real question becomes not a matter of the broad masses somehow reforming the Party, but who's going to control the party from within. The Cultural Revolution from that point on largely becomes a conflict over Party control. This process culminates in April 1969, at the ninth Congress of the Chinese Communist Party. At that point, it's pretty clear that Mao and his followers have achieved sufficient control within the Party; and although the official Cultural Revolution, the Cultural Revolution in name, continues all the way down until Mao's death in 1976, practically speaking, the active political phase of the Cultural Revolution comes to an end in the spring of 1969.

The final seven years of Mao's life were characterized by a functional stalemate within the Party leadership. Mao's group, particularly a quartet of radical leaders called the Gang of Four, with Mao's wife Jiang Qing as their principal leader, came to control much of the Party's propaganda and education and cultural institutions; but other supposed allies of Mao, supposed successors to Mao—most notably Lin Biao, who was supposed to be the man who would take over for Mao after his death—wind up being denounced as a traitors, and [Lin] dies in a plane crash trying to flee China after supposedly having plotted to assassinate Mao. The Maoist side of the conflict within the Party is, to some extent, in disarray.

The pragmatists, on the other hand, find themselves staging something of a comeback. Liu Shaoqi, the leader of this grouping originally, dies in 1969, but Deng Xiaoping, who was his second-in-command, having been purged not just once but several times, makes a return to power, particularly after 1972, and is in fact put in charge of science and technology policy for China. Through the early '70s, it appears that Mao is balancing off the radicals like the Gang of Four against the pragmatists like Deng Xiaoping. Having decided to retain the central role of the Chinese Communist Party, he now is stuck with this situation of not being able to resolve the conflicts within the party, and this makes the last phase of Mao's leadership really a tragic and rather pathetic period; 1976 proves to be the critical year. It is the year in which Mao himself will die, but that is in some ways only the end of a series of quite dramatic events.

In January, Zhou Enlai, who was perhaps the most popular leader amongst the Communists up to this point—he had been prime minister since the establishment of the People's Republic back in 1949—Zhou Enlai dies. His death is widely mourned, and in April of 1976, people in Beijing go to Tiananmen Square and put flowers, other kinds of memorials at the Monument to the People's Heroes. This is interpreted by the Gang of Four, the radical wing of the party, as a criticism of them. Zhou Enlai had always remained very close to Mao, but he had never really endorsed or supported the more radical activities of the Gang of Four, and they saw him as, in fact, having been their enemy, being an adversary. So when popular support, popular admiration for Zhou was expressed, they interpreted this as a popular attack on them, and there's quite a confrontation at Tiananmen in April of '76, and riots break out, some police cars are overturned and burned, and troops have to be sent in to quiet the situation down. It doesn't get out of control anywhere near to the degree that things do in 1989, but it does represent the most serious public expression of opposition to the existing leadership that has been seen in China in quite a while.

In July of 1976, a major earthquake centered at a place called Tangshan, northeast of Beijing, kills nearly 300,000 people and causes widespread damage around north China, including in Beijing itself. An earthquake like this, under the traditional cosmological worldview of imperial China and still in popular consciousness, an earthquake like this is an omen, a portent of very serious, very negative impending events. Shortly after the Tangshan earthquake, Zhu De, who had been the founder of the Red Army, dies also, and then finally, on September 9, Mao Zedong himself dies. So 1976 is a year in which three of the founding leaders of the Communist movement pass from the scene, in which a serious public demonstration against the existing leadership takes place in the heart of Beijing, and in which an earthquake frightens not only the people, but the leadership as well.

Almost immediately after Mao's death, the pragmatic wing within the party starts to move against his more radical followers. By early October, the Gang of Four are arrested, and the machinery begins to go to work for the final return of Deng Xiaoping to leadership and to preside over a fairly complete reorientation of the Chinese Communist Party, and of China's course of development in the modern world. In our final lecture, we will turn to the situation of China after Mao, to China at the beginning of a new century, and we will see where China stands as we move into the future.

Lecture Thirty-Six
China and the World in a New Century

Scope:

Mao's death in September 1976 was quickly followed by the abandonment of his revolutionary vision and by a reorientation of China's economic and political development. In the 1980s, Deng Xiaoping led China to adopt an aggressive program of modernization and openness to the outside world. Economic changes gave rise to widespread corruption and unequal access to opportunity, with the members of the Party gaining disproportionate wealth and power. The student-led protests of 1989 vented deep social grievances. Yet despite the violence of their suppression, the CCP has retained legitimacy in the eyes of most Chinese because it has continued to deliver a rising standard of living for the vast majority of the people. As China enters the 21st century and the World Trade Organization, it is perhaps on the threshold of regaining its traditional place as one of the great powers of the world.

Outline

I. Within two years of Mao's death, Deng Xiaoping remerged as the top leader in China.

    A. In October 1976, just a month after Mao died, the members of the Gang of Four were arrested.

        1. A coalition of pragmatists and conservative Party leaders moved to isolate and remove the last of the radical elements.

        2. Mao's designated successor, Hua Guofeng, held on to office, but real power began to flow to Deng.

        3. Military leaders and the technocrats in the state-planning apparatus supported Deng's return to leadership.

        4. In November 1978, Deng was named vice premier, and his control over policy making was assured.

    B. The political and economic orientation of China changed as Mao's policies were abandoned.

        1. Deng wanted to emphasize technical expertise over political considerations.

        2. He began to dismantle collective ownership in agriculture.

3. He adopted strong family-planning measures to bring population growth under control.
4. He expanded opportunities for private economic activity.
5. China opened its doors to direct foreign investment.

II. The 1980s was a great period of development, as China became more engaged with the global economy, but stresses also built up domestically.

   A. As foreign capital flowed into China, the economy began to grow rapidly.
      1. Special Economic Zones were set up to encourage investment.
      2. Market reforms began to be introduced in both agriculture and industry.
      3. Private enterprises grew in number, but Party and government oversight created many opportunities for corruption.

   B. A new strata of wealthy entrepreneurs began to emerge, often with links to the Party, while many workers in state enterprises saw their incomes stagnate.
      1. As some Chinese became wealthier, they began to engage in conspicuous consumption.
      2. Workers in some state sectors, especially in education and professions, did not share in the rising wage scales of private-sector workers.
      3. Public perceptions of growing inequities and corruption began to create social tensions.

III. In 1989, student-led protests challenged the leadership of the CCP.

   A. Protests had taken place throughout the 1980s, especially from 1986 on.
      1. Some of these took the form of anti-Japanese demonstrations.
      2. Others more directly criticized the Party leadership.
      3. Some Party leaders, such as Hu Yaobang, quietly supported such protests.

   B. When Hu died in April 1989, students used his funeral as a forum to launch new protests.
      1. The visit of the reformist Russian leader Gorbachev gave protesters access to the global media.

2. The CCP leadership was taken by surprise by the extent of the demonstrations in Beijing.
3. Deep divisions in the leadership delayed any effective response, positive or negative.
4. When Deng Xiaoping finally resolved to suppress the demonstrations, the use of force was unavoidable.

C. On June 4, the army regained control of Beijing, but hundreds of people were killed in the process.
1. Most students had given up their occupation of Tiananmen Square.
2. The majority of people in central Beijing were from out of town and had nowhere else to go.
3. Fighting in the streets was brief but intense.
4. Beijing was placed under martial law.

IV. In the years since 1989, the CCP has managed to maintain its legitimacy by delivering rising living standards, but the need for eventual political change cannot be ignored forever.

A. China is, today, perhaps the most rapidly developing country in the world.
1. The economy continues to grow at exceptionally fast rates.
2. Hundreds of millions of Chinese have seen dramatic improvements in their material conditions of life.
3. But problems have also grown in health care and education, as well as other social services.
4. The Marriage Law of 1950 was a strong effort to equalize the status of men and women in Chinese society. In the era of economic reform, however, the status of women has deteriorated.
5. Crime, while still much less of a problem than in the West, has been growing.

B. On the threshold of the 21st century, China is poised for continuing growth and is likely to resume its ancient role as a great world power.
1. Although China has undergone dramatic and often traumatic change in the modern age, it has also retained strong links to its past.
2. In the post-Communist age, many elements of traditional society have begun to reemerge.

3. Even Confucian values are finding new life in today's China.
4. How China will assume its place in the world in the decades ahead remains unclear, but there can be little doubt that it will be a force to be reckoned with.
5. Understanding China's long and complex history is important, not only for its inherent interest, but for each of us as participants in the public life of our country and our world.

Essential Reading:

Bruce Gilley, *Tiger on the Brink*.

Supplemental Reading:

Roderick MacFarquhar, ed., *The Politics of China: The Eras of Mao and Deng*.

Jun Jing, *The Temple of Memories*.

Questions to Consider:

1. How will China's historical experience of the last 200 years shape its relationship with the West in the future?
2. Based on China's role in East Asia and the world in the past, is there any reason to anticipate that China will be a militarily expansionist power?

Lecture Thirty-Six—Transcript
China and the World in a New Century

With the death of Mao Zedong in September of 1976, China reaches yet another turning point, this one resulting within two years in the return of Deng Xiaoping now as the supreme leader in China, the triumph of the pragmatist wing within the Communist Party, and the launching of China on a new road of modernization and development. The socialist path that had been followed under Mao's leadership comes to be largely abandoned, and China places itself—ironically, as Mao had predicted—on the capitalist road, and since that time has achieved tremendous growth and development which now, at the beginning of the 21st century, positions China to once again a resume a leading role economically, politically in the world of the future.

Events moved very quickly after Mao's death. In October 1976, just a month after Mao had passed on, a coalition of pragmatists, conservative party leaders, and military leaders came together to isolate and remove Mao's radical followers. Mao's designated successor, a man named Hua Guofeng, who was from Mao's home province of Hunan, had a relatively undistinguished career in public security services, but had been named by Mao as his successor, Hua Guofeng holds on to office for a while after Mao's death, but there's nothing really to distinguish him. He doesn't have a particular vision or dynamism of his own, and what's at work is the process of bringing Deng Xiaoping back into the leadership. Military leaders, technocrats in the state planning apparatus, were among Deng's strongest supporters, and in November of 1978, a Party gathering names Deng Xiaoping as vice premier and assures his control over policy making.

Deng then sets about carefully—not with excessive haste, but nonetheless quite clearly and relentlessly—to reorient China's policies, China's entire development strategy. The technical expertise of planners, of managers, of Party leaders is emphasized over their political characterization. He begins to pursue the dismantling of collective ownership, particularly in agriculture. He adopts measures for family planning. Family planning had been quite a contentious issue. Mao had believed that more babies meant more workers, and more workers meant more Communists and so therefore family planning was a bad idea. Deng Xiaoping now begins to institute population control efforts, recognizing that a continued rapid expansion of China's population would eat up whatever benefits economic development might create. He begins to expand opportunities for economic activity in the private sector. Perhaps most significantly, Deng Xiaoping puts into high gear policies, which in some ways had already begun under Mao. It was Mao, after all, who had welcomed President Nixon to China back in 1972, and had begun the process of allowing China to open more to the outside world.

Deng Xiaoping now puts this much higher on his list of priorities and accelerates the pace of China's opening to the outside world. In particular, he begins to welcome direct foreign investment in the Chinese economy, at first in very careful, controlled ways, but as time goes by, in an increasingly open embrace of the global economy. As foreign capital begins to come into China, the economy starts to expand really quite rapidly. At first, special economic zones are created, in a way echoing all the way back to Qing policy; and special economic zones, when they first are to be set up, are created far away in the south, far from the political center in Beijing. Two of the earliest special economic zones are created just outside of Hong Kong. So back in the far south, where the old Canton system had been centered, now we have the first of the special economic zones going in. But as their success becomes evident, they're established elsewhere, and eventually all of China in effect becomes a special economic zone, with foreign investment and foreign economic activity playing an increasing role in China's growth and development.

Domestically, market reforms begin to be introduced both in agriculture and in industry. In agriculture, experiments with breaking up agricultural collectives, not granting formal legal titles to land, but giving farming households very long-term leases—initially 15-20 years, eventually these start to be 99-year leases—in effect creating a system of private property in the countryside. These are developed in conjunction with what's called the "contract system," under which agricultural households will enter into an agreement with government purchasing units to supply a certain amount of grain or vegetables or whatever agricultural commodities are involved, and whatever surplus they have beyond that contract with the state, they can sell on the private market. This rapidly leads to expansion of agricultural production and the flourishing of the private sector in the agricultural economy.

Private industrial enterprises also begin to grow, and when I characterize these as private, that's perhaps an overstatement. They are not public state sector enterprises, but many of them are in practice only semi-private to begin with. They are enterprises that are started not by the Ministry of Machine Building or the Ministry of the Electronics Industry or something like that, but by local level collective or cooperative units. Sometimes these are township governments, sometimes these may be county governments, sometimes they are public and private partnerships, but they are new forms of organization, new forms of the economic institutions, and they become very dynamic. Growth in this private and semi-private component of the economy rapidly outstrips what's taking place in a public sector, and these become the most dynamic enterprises in China.

Nonetheless, problems go along with this. Because of the heritage of socialism, and because of the central role of the Chinese Communist Party, the process of transforming the economy, both institutionally and in terms of the actual allocation of resources, is one which comes to be distorted by the role of the Party, and to some extent of the state machine, but the Party's perhaps most important here. Because to operate a private venture, or to operate one of these mixed public-private enterprises, different kinds of permits or licenses will need to be acquired; and to get permission for those, the Party Secretary or the Party officer of a particular government unit has to approve; and so, opportunities for corruption, for bribery, for getting shares of equity perhaps in a new company as a favor for the people in the Party who have to grant approval, these become characteristic, and corruption becomes a significant component of the economic growth and development that takes place. As we'll see shortly, concern about this, frustration with this, resentment about this, becomes a very significant political issue.

There are other consequences of economic growth and modernization that begin to manifest themselves as we move through the 1980s. Some parts of the economy, private enterprises, public-private partnerships, joint ventures between Chinese enterprises and foreign investments, begin to grow and flourish. Incomes rise, wealth is being created, a more prosperous middle class begins to emerge.

But other sectors of the economy don't benefit, or don't benefit as much as these. For example, in the state sector, on the one hand you have the massive industrial enterprises—steel mills, automobile factories, and the railway system—these remain under state control. They're not very profitable in a sort of classic economic sense, and yet their position in the Chinese economy and social system are vital because they employ tens of millions, probably hundreds of millions of workers, and they provide a whole network of social services—educational services, health services, retirement services—which would otherwise have to be picked up by the government itself. The reform of the state sector becomes a serious problem, a set of contradictions, a set of tensions pulling in different directions.

Some of the state enterprises manage to adapt a bit and become more profitable, more rationalized in an economic sense, and remain competitive. Others tend to stagnate and operate on a "business as usual" basis. But even there, the government is able to put some additional investment in and raise standards of living, raise income levels—not perhaps keeping up entirely with the private and semi-private sectors, but at least not falling too far behind. Other areas of public employment, most particularly things like education, the health care service, stagnate. Wages don't rise, working conditions don't improve, housing conditions don't improve, and teachers, professionals of various types, begin to feel left out, begin to feel that they're being left behind as China moves forward with its economic development. They're particularly resentful when they see members of the Party—and often the sons and daughters of Party leaders—benefiting disproportionately, not from the hard work that they're putting in, but simply from taking advantage of their position within these privileged institutions.

This public perception of growing inequities and corruption becomes more and more of the source of social tension as we move through the 1980s. In 1989, this reaches a serious crisis point, and we see a very public challenge to the continued authority and leadership of the Chinese Communist Party. All through the '80s, and particularly from 1986 on, there had been small-scale, localized demonstrations of protest, of frustration. Some of these were in the form of anti-Japanese protests. The hostility between China and Japan, the lingering legacy of events like the Rape of Nanjing, are still part of popular consciousness in China, even among young people today; and the opening of China to the outside world, the influx of outside investment, some of that was coming from Japan, and the Japanese became a convenient target. Frustration with economic change, frustration with the corruption within the Chinese system could be vented in the form of anti-Japanese political actions. Those took place a number of times in the mid-1980s.

Other demonstrations, other protest movements criticized the Party leadership more directly. Some outspoken intellectual figures came to be quite prominent in their criticism and challenging of the Party leadership. At the same time, within the Party leadership, there were individuals who began to emerge as more sympathetic to these protests. A reform wing, or perhaps a more rapid reform wing, begins to be discernible within the Party leadership. These debates are now a little bit more public, a little more easy to observe than they had been back in the '50s or '60s; and we know that individuals such as Hu Yaobang or Zhao Ziyang and came to be advocates of more rapid reform, more liberalization, more opportunities for the participation of ordinary people in the political process. Hu Yaobang, who had become very popular in this role, and who had in fact been disciplined to some extent by the Party leadership for being maybe a little too outspoken, dies in April of 1989. His death, echoing back to the death of Zhou Enlai in 1976, and the popular demonstrations which had followed it, Hu Yaobang's death becomes the spark, the starting point for the student protests and the mass demonstrations in Beijing in the spring of 1989.

A number of factors come together at this time to make this a dynamic and potentially explosive situation. Hu Yaobang's death leads to the outpouring of public sentiment in support of him, in favor of more reform, more liberalization. Almost at the same time, just a matter of a week or two later, the Russian Reformist leader Gorbachev was making a visit to China, and the Chinese leadership was very proud of this, to have the Russian leader coming to China. This was seen in some ways as recognition of China's success, of the status that China was achieving, and the Chinese leadership is very proud of this. When Gorbachev arrives, student demonstrators occupy Tiananmen Square, and it's impossible to bring Gorbachev for the big ceremonial welcome at the Great Hall of the people. This is a humiliation, an embarrassment for the Party leadership, and this begins to turn them against whatever sympathies they might have had for the student demonstrations.

The leadership still remains divided. Debates take place within the very top levels of the Party over how to respond. Should they impose martial law? Some articles are published in the papers denouncing the student demonstrators as anti-revolutionary. Other forces within the leadership want to have a more sympathetic line towards the students. The Western media gets involved, of course, and outside reporters start to talk about to this as threatening the overthrow, threatening the collapse of the government, threatening the end of the rule of the Chinese Communist Party. Of course, from the point of view of the Western media, this was a desirable outcome, but for the Communist leadership to be hearing this on the world news only made them more determined to hold on to the existing status.

It is ultimately Deng Xiaoping who resolves this conflict. He decides, in some ways reminiscent of Mao's decision to maintain the leadership of the Party during the Cultural Revolution, Deng decides that the demonstrations have to be suppressed, and that force will be used as needed to do so. That decision is critical to his view of how China is to go forward. Deng Xiaoping was a believer in pragmatism, in the leadership of experts, of technicians. He wasn't necessarily a great advocate of popular participatory democracy, and we can see that in this instance, his fear of unrest, his fear of instability, of potential chaos, far outweighed his desire to have popular support for reform. He wanted to modernize China, he wanted to make China a wealthy and powerful country, but he didn't necessarily want to allow that process to be guided by forces outside of the Chinese Communist Party.

On June 4 of 1989, the forces of the People's Liberation Army move into Beijing. There are very dramatic and violent confrontations between people in the streets of the city and these military forces coming in from the east and west. Certainly hundreds of people are killed in the fighting that night, and eventually the troops reach Tiananmen Square. A negotiated agreement is reached to get the last of the students holding out in the Square to leave, which they do. Many of them are pursued and arrested in later days, although many of them also manage to escape and flee to the west. Martial law is in place in Beijing, and this challenge, this movement to confront the government, to repudiate the corruption, the inequities that are emerging in the course of economic reform, and to call for greater popular participation, is brought to an end.

In 1989, in the summer of 1989 many people looking at China thought that they were in a very serious crisis, that the leadership of the Communist Party had been permanently undermined, that China's ability to continue to attract foreign investment, and thereby to continue to pursue its course of economic development, was going to be seriously curtailed, and that the future looked rather bleak, both for the Chinese Communist leadership and for the people of China. In the years since 1989, the actual course of events has proved to be rather different. The Chinese Communist Party has managed to maintain its leadership, and to a significant extent to maintain its legitimacy. It is still accepted, perhaps not overwhelmingly loved and admired, but certainly respected by the vast majority of the Chinese people.

The foundation for this is really very straightforward, which is the capacity of the Chinese leadership to deliver steadily improving material standards of living and steadily increasing degrees of individual freedom to the Chinese people. China today is perhaps the most rapidly developing country in the world. Certainly, of any countries of any significant size, it is the most rapidly developing country in the world. The Chinese economy continues to grow at exceptionally fast rates; average growth over the years, over the last 20-25 years, has been over 7 percent. This year's growth rate is anticipated to be over 9 percent. The leadership recently announced that they were going to try to cool things off next year in the future by reducing growth to only 7 percent. Most countries would be delighted to have 7 percent growth, and the idea that this represents a conservative turn for China only indicates how rapid their overall development has been.

The economic growth of China has lifted the material standards of living for hundreds of millions of people. Between 1990 and 2001, almost 300 million Chinese had their incomes raise enough to place them above the United Nations' poverty level. There are still over 100 million Chinese living below the United Nations' poverty line, but no country in history has ever lifted so many people out of poverty in so short a time. These achievements of growth, of development in China are truly phenomenal. Most recently perhaps, the dynamism of China, China's ability to become a modern country has been demonstrated by their launching of a man into outer space, the first orbital flights by Chinese astronaut in a Chinese space vehicle. This technological achievement was, of course, wildly welcomed in China, and is seen by the Chinese as a demonstration of their return to prosperity, to stability and to a place of significance in the world.

These achievements, however, have not come without considerable cost. The problems that were often associated with the old China—certainly with the China of the middle years of the 20th century, problems of health care, problems of disease, problems of crime, problems of drug addiction, problems relating to the status of women—many of these issues which had gone away to a considerable extent during the 1950s, 1960s, and 1970s, are now with us once again in China. A function, certainly at least a byproduct of the economic reform programs that have given China tremendous growth, have also meant that social services have deteriorated.

The educational sector has gone from one in which the goal was universal public education and expanding higher education for high school graduates—China was far from achieving its objectives but was moving steadily in that direction—to one in which the public education sector has stagnated. Funding for schools is grossly inadequate, teacher salaries have not risen in anywhere near parity with the rest of the economy, and this has become so much a problem in China, that in the cities, wealthy families, of which there is a largely and rapidly growing supply, are sending their children to private schools. A two-tier system of education, a publicly funded—but not very adequately funded—system of schools on the one hand, and a private school system where the children of the new middle class, the well-off urban sector can achieve really very good education; so, a movement away from the egalitarian ideas of socialism and the building of a new China to a system much more similar to the capitalist economies of the Western world.

Health care has gone in quite comparable directions. One of the great achievements of the cultural revolution was the system of what were called barefoot doctors, people who weren't really highly sophisticated or very highly trained or educated medical practitioners, but who had basic skills in disease prevention and popular health services who would go anywhere in the country, who often lived out in the countryside, who practiced in the poorest villages. This was again an ideal which was not necessarily fully realized, but which was the dominant mode of investment and development under the socialist regime. The health care system has become again much more like the Western health care system. Hospitals are expensive places to go, health insurance is in short supply, hospitals increasingly invest in high-tech medical equipment, which makes their service costs much higher, and health too has become something which is now available with a great deal of differential based upon incomes. Economic growth has also resulted in economic inequality, and that has resulted in a deterioration of services for many people.

The situation of women, finally, is one, which has been very problematic. The Marriage Law of 1950 was a very strong effort to equalize the status of men and women in Chinese society, to provide women with the kinds of economic resources necessary to ensure that their status was substantive and not merely putative. In the era of economic reform, the status of women has deteriorated quite significantly. When factories have been rationalized, the employees laid off first have tended to be the women. The ideal of women remaining at home, taking care of domestic tasks without, of course, being paid, has become the norm again, certainly in urban China. Educational opportunities for women have declined, particularly in the private sector. This is not to say that there are not women being educated, but that the extent to which this is an egalitarian system has declined significantly. In the countryside, practices of arranged marriages, kidnapping women by marriage, matrimonial agents, bride prices, dowries, many of the abuses associated with the old society have also returned.

We're now on the threshold of the 21st century, moving into the early years of the century. It's a period where China's growth almost certainly will continue. There will be problems, there will be challenges which China will face; but it seems highly likely that as the century progresses, China will return to the position of power, prestige, world leadership which it traditionally occupied In many ways, the last two centuries since the end of the 18th century have been an anomaly. As we've looked over the long sweep of Chinese history, we've seen that there have been periods of growth and dynamism, and periods of decline and fragmentation. In the long term, historians of the future will look back on the 20th century as an era of fragmentation and on the 21st as a period when China returned to its former glory. It's been a pleasure working with you through these lectures. Good day.

Map

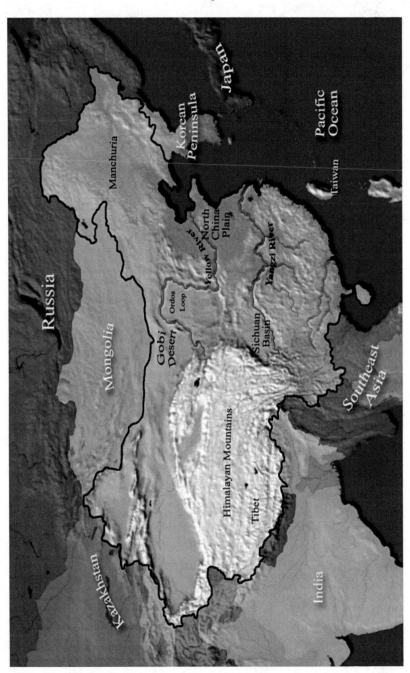

Timeline

c. 500,000 B.C.E. ....Peking Man hominid fossils.

c. 10,000 B.C.E. ....Domestication of rice in Jiangxi.

c. 4600 B.C.E. ....Neolithic village cultures in northern China.

c. 2100 B.C.E. ....Xia "dynasty" in Yellow River valley.

c. 1500 B.C.E. ....Shang state on North China Plain.

1045 B.C.E. ....Zhou Conquest.

722–481 B.C.E. ....Spring and Autumn period.

480–221 B.C.E. ....Warring States period.

207 B.C.E. ....Fall of Qin dynasty.

202 B.C.E.–220 C.E. ....Han dynasty.

141–87 B.C.E. ....Reign of Wudi.

81 B.C.E. ....Debate on Salt and Iron.

9–23 C.E. ....Usurpation of Wang Mang.

c. 100 C.E. ....First Buddhist temple in China.

182 C.E. ....Yellow Turban uprising.

220–280 ....Three Kingdoms period.

c. 310 ....Turkic migrations into northern China begin.

581–618 ....Sui dynasty.

618–906 ....Tang dynasty.

684–705 ....Reign of Empress Wu Zetian.

713–756 ....Reign of Xuanzong.

755–763 ....An Lushan rebellion.

768–824 ....Han Yu.

845 ....Official suppression of Buddhism.

907–960...Five Dynasties period.

907–1125......................................Liao dynasty of the Khitan people.

960–1127......................................Northern Song dynasty.

1126–1234....................................Jin dynasty of the Jurchen people.

1127–1279....................................Southern Song dynasty.

1130–1200....................................Zhu Xi.

1206 ....Mongol *quriltai* elects Temujin as Great Khan.

1260–1368....................................Mongol Yuan dynasty.

1272–1290....................................Marco Polo in China.

1313 ....Mongols restore Confucian examinations.

1340s...Great plague in Yangzi River valley.

1368–1644 ....Ming dynasty.

1402 ....Zhu Di usurps the throne.

1405–1435....................................Ming voyages of exploration.

1572–1620....................................Reign of Wanli emperor.

c. 1580..."Single Whip" tax reforms.

1626 ....Nurhaci inaugurates Manchu language use.

1636 ....Qing dynasty proclaimed by Manchus.

1644 ....Fall of Ming dynasty and Manchu invasion.

1661–1722....................................Reign of Kangxi.

1673–1681....................................Rebellion of the Wu Sangui.

1712 ....Kangxi's tax edict.

1723–1735....................................Reign of Yongzheng.

1736–1795....................................Reign of Qianlong.

1793	British trade mission to China.
1813	Secret society rebellion against Qing.
1839–1842	Opium War.
1850–1864	Taiping Rebellion.
1864–1895	Self-Strengthening Movement.
1894–1895	Sino-Japanese War.
1898	100 Days Reforms.
1899–1900	Boxer Rebellion.
1905	Confucian examinations abolished.
October 11, 1911	Wuhan mutiny sets off revolution.
February 12, 1912	Abdication of last emperor.
February 15, 1912	Yuan Shikai becomes president.
1916	Yuan Shikai tries to become emperor.
May 4, 1919	Student demonstration in Beijing.
July 1921	Founding of Chinese Communist Party.
1922–1927	First United Front of Communists and Nationalists.
1926	Northern Expedition of Chiang Kaishek.
April 1927	Split between CCP and GMD.
1929–1934	Jiangxi period of Chinese Communists.
September 18, 1931	Japanese invade Manchuria.
October 1934–October 1935	Long March.
December 1936	Xian incident: Chiang "arrested."
1937–1945	Second United Front.

July 7, 1937 ....Marco Polo Bridge incident: Japanese invasion.

1945 ....End of war with Japan.

1945–1949 ....Civil war between Communists and Nationalists.

1948 ....Nationalists massacre Taiwanese.

1949 ....Nationalists withdraw to Taiwan.

October 1, 1949 ....Mao proclaims People's Republic of China.

1949–1952 ....Land reform.

1950 ....Marriage law.

1958–1959 ....Great Leap Forward.

August 1959 ....Lushan Plenum: Peng Dehuai purged, Mao retreats from daily leadership.

1962 ....Socialist Education Movement.

1966–1969 ....Great Proletarian Cultural Revolution.

1976 ....Death of Mao Zedong.

1978–1994 ....Leadership of Deng Xiaoping.

1989 ....Tiananmen student movement, suppressed June 4.

1999 ....China and the United States agree on WTO membership.

Glossary

Boxers: Mystical peasant movement originating in Shandong province in the late 1890s. Members believed that they were immune to Western weapons because of special chants and talismans. Opposed to Christian missionaries and the power of the Western nations over China.

Cohong system: System developed in the 18th century to regulate and control trade with Western merchants. Trade was restricted to the port of Canton (Guangzhou) in the far south. Western traders had to work with Chinese brokers and could not trade directly with Chinese merchants.

Confucianism: Based on the teaching of Confucius and Mencius, this became the official ideology of the imperial state from the Han dynasty on. Confucian doctrine emphasized social relationships, ritual, and learning.

Dao: Literally, a path or road and, by extension, "the Way." The ideal of a well-ordered society, whether by human design or by natural pattern. Also used in Buddhism to signify the spiritual path.

Daoism: The philosophy based on the teachings of Laozi and Zhuangzi, emphasizing skeptical views about knowledge and action and promoting harmony with natural order. Later became a more religious movement with a strong mystical dimension focused on the quest for immortality.

Daoxue: Literally, the "Learning of the Way." The metaphysical interpretation of Confucianism that developed during the Song dynasty and was given its mature form by Zhu Xi.

Dynasty: A period of time during which a single family controlled the throne and the succession of rulership.

Gang of Four: Radical followers of Mao Zedong in the 1970s who pushed an anti-bureaucratic vision for the Chinese Communist Party. Led by Mao's wife, Jiang Qing, it also included Yao Wenyuan, Zhang Chunqiao, and Wang Hongwen.

Great Leap Forward: Mass mobilization campaign in 1958–1959 aiming to dramatically increase China's agricultural and industrial output. The People's Communes were the main organizational form, in which tens of thousands of farming households were joined into single accounting and decision-making units. The Great Leap collapsed when misreporting of harvests led to over-consumption of grain; faulty planning and bad weather also greatly reduced yields and led to widespread food shortages.

Guwen: Literally, "old-style writing." A literary reform movement in the later Tang dynasty, largely led by Han Yu (768–824). It was part of a revival of Confucian values and a critical reevaluation of the place of Buddhism in China.

Land reform: The seizure and redistribution of land between 1948 and 1952 designed to eliminate the old system of land tenure, in which a small elite held much of the land while many farming families had none at all. Land was distributed to all peasants, male and female. These actions combined to break the power of the landlord class over rural society and created the basis for expanding agricultural production.

Legalism: A philosophical system closely associated with the state of Qin during the Warring States period. Legalism was based on a system of rewards and punishments. Laws and regulations were established by the state, and anyone who violated them, whether high official or lowly peasant, would be punished equally.

Li ("pattern/principle"): A fundamental concept in Neo-Confucian thought. By observing natural patterns, one can discern the underlying principles of the operation of the universe. Good or proper actions are those that are in harmony with natural patterns, while evil consists in transgressing or violating them.

Li ("ritual"): Ritual is the system of gestures and roles that structures and facilitates social interactions. It can be as simple as bowing or shaking hands when meeting someone or as elaborate as an imperial sacrifice or the recognition of successful examination candidates, involving thousands of participants in complex performances.

Literati: The educated elite, from which came the officials who staffed the imperial bureaucracy. Membership in the literati was based on educational accomplishment, but because this required certain economic resources to achieve, the literati tended to be an economic elite, as well.

Long March: The epic journey of the Chinese Communist Party and the Red Army from Jiangxi in the southeast to Shaanxi in the northwest between October 1934 and October 1935. Of the 115,000 people who set out, only about 15,000 survived the journey. They were regarded as heroes of the revolution ever after.

Mandate of Heaven: The central concept of legitimacy in the traditional political culture. Heaven, which is something like an organic operating system, bestows the Mandate on a particular individual and his descendants, as long as they rule in the general interests of society. If the rulers become cruel and abusive, Heaven will withdraw the Mandate, the dynasty will be overthrown, and a new dynasty will be established by whoever receives the Mandate.

May 4th Movement: Student demonstrations in Beijing in 1919 to protest the perceived betrayal of China by the Versailles Peace Conference after World War I, which allowed Japan to keep the former German territorial concessions in Shandong. The movement spread to anti-Japanese boycotts and strikes across China and helped galvanize a new age of revolutionary activity.

Moism: The teachings of the Warring States thinker Mozi. Mozi emphasized a doctrine of "universal love," in contrast to what he saw as the family-centered teachings of Confucius. Mozi also sought to render the aggressive warfare of the Warring States period unprofitable by developing and sharing techniques of defense.

Neo-Confucianism: The English term generally used for the ideas of *Daoxue*. In English, the emphasis is on the new and innovative aspects of *Daoxue*, while the Chinese have seen it as a more retrospective doctrine, in line with traditional Confucian concepts of reverence for the past.

New Culture Movement: Cultural movement of the 1910s and 1920s that rejected the "dead weight" of traditional culture, especially Confucianism and the imperial state. Its members promoted the use of vernacular language in writing and began the process of simplifying the writing of Chinese characters.

Quriltai: The grand assembly of the Mongol tribes that could elect a Great Khan. It did not meet regularly but could be convened by anyone with sufficient following among the Mongols. Temujin convened a *quriltai* in 1206, at which he had himself proclaimed Chinggis Khan, which means "Oceanic Ruler."

Shi: The administrative elite that emerged during the Zhou dynasty. Initially made up of men appointed to work at the many local courts, the *shi* changed over time into a landholding semi-aristocratic elite during Han-Tang times and into the educationally based elite of the late imperial age from the Song on.

Single Whip reforms: A set of changes to the fiscal and revenue policies of the Ming dynasty in the 1580s. The main result was that taxes were paid in silver rather than in grain or cloth, as had been the case. This benefited the commercially advanced coastal and riverine provinces but set the stage for problems in the arid northwest and the rugged hills of the southwest.

Spring and Autumn period: The period, from the mid-8th through the early 5th centuries B.C.E., when the central authority of the Zhou kings began to decline. Named for the historical records of the state of Lu, which were later believed to have been edited by Confucius.

Taiping: Literally, "Great Peace," this term is also shorthand for the Taiping Tianguo, or the Heavenly Kingdom of Great Peace. This was the rebel state created by Hong Xiuquan between 1850 and 1864, which controlled much of central and south China and ruled over, perhaps, 100 million people.

Warring States period: A prolonged period of chronic warfare and insecurity from the 5th through the late 3rd centuries B.C.E. Stronger states slowly conquered weaker ones until only a few remained in the 3rd century. Finally, the state of Qin defeated the last of its rivals, destroying the southern kingdom of Chu in 221 B.C.E.

Biographical Notes

Abaoji (r. 907–926): Founder of the Liao dynasty of the Khitan people on the northern frontier of China following the collapse of the Tang dynasty.

An Lushan (d. 757): Turkic military commander for the Tang army garrison at modern Beijing. He was a favorite of the emperor Xuanzong but came under suspicion of an illicit relationship with the emperor's favorite concubine, Yang Guifei. Led a major rebellion in 755.

Cao Cao (155–220): Late Han general whose military genius became legendary. Father of Cao Pei, who founded the Kingdom of Wei at the beginning of the Three Kingdoms period.

Chen Duxiu (1879–1942): Intellectual leader of the May 4th Movement and early advocate of Marxism. Helped found the Chinese Communist Party in 1921, though he did not attend the First Congress in Shanghai.

Cheng Hao/Cheng Yi (1032–1085/1033–1107): Brothers who were early advocates of the ideas that developed into *Daoxue* Neo-Confucianism in the Song dynasty.

Chiang Kaishek (1888–1975): Military leader and strongman of the Guomindang Nationalist Party from 1926 until his death. Strongly anti-Communist, he directed Nationalist forces primarily against the CCP, rather than the Japanese who invaded China in the 1930s. After defeat in the civil war, he led the Nationalist regime on Taiwan.

Cixi (1835–1908): Consort of emperor Xianfeng in the 1850s, she was the mother of the Tongzhi emperor (r. 1860–1872) and, later, as Empress Dowager, was the power behind the throne in the last decades of Manchu rule.

Confucius (551–479 B.C.E.): Political thinker in the Warring States period whose ideas about human relations, ritual, and learning came to be the core ideology of the imperial state.

Deng Xiaoping (1904–1997): Joined the Communist Party as a student in France in the 1920s. Later returned to China and took part in the Long March. Rose to a leading position in the 1950s, then was purged during the Cultural Revolution. Returned to power in 1978 and became supreme leader, guiding the reforms of the 1980s.

Dong Zhongshu (2nd century B.C.E.): Political and cosmological thinker during the reign of Wudi. His ideas about connections between natural phenomena and human actions influenced concepts of legitimacy and succession for the imperial state.

Duke of Zhou (11th century B.C.E.): Uncle and chief advisor of King Wu at the time of the founding of the Zhou dynasty. He became the model of the sage advisor, the ideal for the later *shi* administrative elite.

Fan Kuan (active c. 1023–1031): Landscape painter during the Northern Song dynasty. His depictions of massive mountains with tiny human figures in marginal positions typified the changing view of man and nature in the 11th century.

Gu Kaizhi (c. 345–c. 406): First identifiable painter in China. Several paintings attributed to him survive but most are probably slightly later copies.

Guangxu (1871–1908): Next-to-last emperor of the Qing. Dominated by his great aunt, the Empress Dowager Cixi, he began to rule in his own right in the mid-1890s. His support for reform in the summer of 1898 led to his house arrest in September. He died in 1908 on the eve of Cixi's death, leading to speculation that he was poisoned.

Han Fei (d. 233 B.C.E.): Philosopher of the state of Qin. He developed a sophisticated rationale for the Legalist doctrines of rewards and punishments. Han Fei argued that human nature was a blank slate and that, by use of rewards and punishments, people could be shaped to be obedient citizens.

Han Yu (768–824): Scholar and official in the late Tang dynasty who promoted a Confucian revival through his advocacy of *guwen*, or "ancient-style," prose writing. He criticized what he saw as the baleful influence of Buddhism on Chinese culture and called for a return to the values of the early Han dynasty.

Hong Xiuquan (1813–1864): Founder and leader of the Taiping Heavenly Kingdom. He was a failed examination candidate from Guangdong province who had visions that he believed to be a revelation that he was the younger brother of Jesus Christ. His movement almost toppled the Qing dynasty, and its suppression cost some 20 million lives.

Hu Yaobang (1915–1989): Communist Party official who rose to be general secretary during the reform period of the 1980s. His death in April 1989 triggered the student movement that culminated in military suppression in June.

Jiang Qing (1914–1999): Wife of Mao Zedong. During the Cultural Revolution, she was responsible for the reform of performing arts. She became the leader of the so-called Gang of Four, who sought to promote a radical vision of egalitarian revolution.

Jiang Zemin (1926–): Communist Party official and former mayor of Shanghai who became general secretary after the suppression of the Tiananmen student movement in June 1989. He restored order and returned to the path of reform and openness to the outside world inaugurated by Deng Xiaoping.

Kang Youwei (1858–1927): Confucian reformer who was one of the leaders of the 100 Days Reforms of 1898. He later became a conservative advocate of a constitutional monarchy.

Kangxi (1654–1722): Second emperor of the Qing dynasty. He presided over the suppression of the rebellion of Wu Sangui and launched campaigns to bring the Mongol tribes of Xinjiang into the Qing Empire. His tax edict of 1712 fixed the fiscal system of the dynasty "in perpetuity."

Khubilai (1214–1294): Grandson of Temujin and first emperor of the Mongol Yuan dynasty in China. He completed the conquest of the Song and established the Mongol capital at Dadu, present-day Beijing.

Laozi (6th century B.C.E.): Semi-legendary philosopher of the Warring States period whose ideas became the foundation for Daoism. He rejected the positivism of Confucian thought and encouraged a skeptical approach to knowledge and action; he also advocated seeking harmony with nature.

Li Dazhao (1889–1927): Educator and radical thinker during the May 4th period. One of the founders of the Communist Party. Killed during the split with Chiang Kaishek in 1927.

Li Shimin (597–649): Second emperor of the Tang dynasty. He encouraged his father, Li Yuan, to rebel against the Sui dynasty and found a new order, then succeeded his father in 626.

Li Zicheng (1606–1645): Leader of a peasant rebellion against the Ming in Shanxi in the early 1640s, he succeeded in capturing Beijing in April 1644. He established a short-lived dynasty of his own but was chased out of the capital by Wu Sangui and the Mongols in early June.

Liang Qichao (1873–1929): Reformer and writer. He was active with Kang Youwei in the 1898 Reforms and, later, became a publisher of radical newspapers in Shanghai and Japan.

Lin Biao (1908–1971): Communist military leader and later minister of defense. He became Mao's designated successor in 1969 but, shortly thereafter, was killed in an apparent split within the radical leadership. He is reported to have attempted to assassinate Mao before fleeing in an airplane, which was shot down over Mongolia.

Lin Zexu (1785–1850): Qing official who was put in charge of opium suppression in Guangzhou in 1838. His strong efforts to eliminate the drug trade led the British to launch the Opium War (1939–1942).

Liu Bang (247–195 B.C.E.): Petty official of the Qin state who rebelled and raised an army that allowed him to establish a new dynasty, the Han, in 202 B.C.E. Reigned as first emperor until his death.

Liu Bei (162–223 C.E.): Descendant in a minor line of the Han imperial family, he founded the state of Shu Han in 220 at the beginning of the Three Kingdoms period.

Liu Shaoqi (1898–1969): Communist Party leader and president of the People's Republic in the 1950s and early 1960s. He became the chief focus of opposition to Mao and was denounced as a "capitalist roader" in the Cultural Revolution, when he was purged from office and imprisoned. Died of cancer while still under arrest.

Mao Zedong (1893–1976): One of the founders of the Communist Party, he became an advocate of the "peasant strategy" in the late 1920s. Became chairman of the Party in 1935 and remained its chief leader until his death.

Marco Polo (1254–1324): Venetian traveler who visited China from c. 1275–1290. He served as an official under Khubilai and left a rich memoir of his travels, which was criticized in Europe as wildly exaggerated.

Mencius (372–289 B.C.E.): Philosopher and interpreter of Confucius. Mencius emphasized the reciprocal nature of social relationships, especially the right of people to overthrow unjust rulers. He also stressed the natural division of society into those who labor with their backs and those who work with their minds.

Mozi (late 5th–early 4th centuries B.C.E.): Warring States period thinker who advocated "universal love" and promoted defensive warfare to make aggression unprofitable.

Nurhaci (1559–1626): Creator of the Manchus. He sought to revive the former Jin dynasty of the Jurchen people and overthrow the Ming dynasty.

Ouyang Xiu (1007–1072): Scholar and official of the Northern Song, he was a representative figure of the "literary gentlemen," who advocated clear prose writing and traditional Confucian values.

Peng Dehuai (1898–1974): Military leader and veteran of the Long March. He led Chinese forces in the Korean War and served as minister of defense in the 1950s. Purged in 1959 for criticizing Mao over the Great Leap Forward.

Puyi (1905–1967): Last emperor of the Qing. He was put on the throne in 1908 at the age of three. Abdicated in 1912. He was later puppet emperor of Manchuguo under the Japanese from 1934–1945.

Qianlong (1711–1799): Fourth emperor of the Qing, he reigned for 60 years, from 1736–1795. Retired in order not to exceed the reign of his grandfather, Kangxi. Qianlong's reign was, in some ways, the high point of the Qing era.

Qinshihuangdi (259–210 B.C.E.): King of the state of Qin at the end of the Warring States, he proclaimed himself First Emperor in 221 B.C.E., when Qin's last rival was defeated. His mausoleum near Xian contains the famous terra cotta warriors.

Shun (c. 2200 B.C.E.): Legendary sage king of antiquity. Named to succeed Emperor Yao, who set aside his own son in favor of Shun's moral uprightness.

Siddhartha (6th century B.C.E.): Indian prince who founded Buddhism. He rejected the material luxury of his life and sought to understand the origins of suffering and how to transcend it.

Sima Guang (1019–1086): Statecraft thinker of the Northern Song. Critic of the reforms of Wang Anshi, he promoted a view of government that emphasized the role of the literati as sage advisors to the emperor.

Su Shi (1037–1101): Scholar, official, and literary theorist. Follower of Ouyang Xiu, he promoted the assimilation of classical literary models as a basis for one's own spontaneous expression.

Sun Quan (181–252): Three Kingdoms ruler of the southeastern state of Wu.

Sun Yatsen (1866–1925): Nationalist revolutionary leader and founder of the Guomindang, the Nationalist Party. Developed the three People's Principles of nationalism, democracy, and socialism.

Sunzi (6th century B.C.E.): Military strategist of the Warring States period. His doctrines of deception and careful preparation became fundamental to Chinese military thinking.

Temujin (c. 1162–1227): Leader of the Mongols in their great age of expansion. Became Chinggis Khan, or Oceanic Ruler, in 1206.

Wang Anshi (1021–1086): Statecraft thinker and political leader. Presided over the reform effort known as the New Policies in the 1070s. Advocated a stronger role for the central government and restriction of the powers of local elites.

Wang Mang (33 B.C.E.–23 C.E.): An official at the Han court, he seized power in 9 C.E. and proclaimed his own dynasty, the Xin. He instituted various reforms, but following his death in 23 C.E., the Liu family reclaimed the throne.

Wang Yangming (1472–1528): Philosopher and official who developed new interpretations of Confucian ideas about knowledge and action. Believed that everyone has an "innate knowledge of the good" and that there was a necessary link between knowing and acting. His ideas have been seen as a Chinese version of individualism and humanism.

King Wen (d. c. 1045 B.C.E.): Last leader of the Zhou people before their overthrow of the Shang. He guided the consolidation of the alliance of subordinate peoples that brought the dynasty to an end.

King Wu (d. c. 1039 B.C.E.): King of the Zhou at the time of the Conquest, he was largely guided by his uncle, the Duke of Zhou.

Wu Sangui (d. 1678): Chinese general who allowed the Manchus to cross the Great Wall in 1644. He was given a large territory to govern in south China but rebelled in 1673 in the last serious challenge to the new dynasty.

Wu Zetian (625–705): Concubine in the harem of Li Shimin, she became empress consort of the next emperor and mother of yet another emperor. In 690, she set aside the Li family and assumed the throne for herself, becoming the only woman ever to rule China in her own name. She abdicated in 705, and the Li family regained the throne and restored the Tang dynasty.

Wudi (r. 142–87 B.C.E.): Dynamic emperor of the Han dynasty, he pursued an activist policy for the state in economic and social life; launched military campaigns to expand the empire; and promoted the synthesis of Confucian, Daoist, and Legalist thought that became the imperial orthodoxy.

Xiang Yu (233–202 B.C.E.): Military leader of the former state of Chu, he joined the rebellion against Qin in 207 B.C.E. and soon became one of the major contenders to found a new dynasty. He was defeated by Liu Bang in 202.

Xuanzong (r. 713–756): Emperor of the Tang, he presided over a long period of growth and stability. Over time, however, he withdrew from active participation in court life and devoted himself to his favorite concubine, Yang Guifei. His jealousy was exploited by officials and led to the rebellion of An Lushan.

Yang Guifei (d. 756): Daughter of an official, she became a consort of the emperor Xuanzong. They became so close that she influenced his decisions on government. Jealous officials alleged an illicit relationship with An Lushan, which led to his rebellion. Yang Guifei was strangled and left by the roadside as the emperor's entourage fled the capital in 756.

Yang Jian (540–605): General who overthrew his emperor and established his own dynasty, the Sui, in 581. He ruled as emperor until his death and was succeeded by his son, Yang Guang.

Yao (c. 2300 B.C.E.): Legendary sage ruler of antiquity. He set aside his own son to appoint Shun as his successor because of his sterling moral qualities.

Yongzheng (1677–1735): Third emperor of the Qing. His attempts to reform the finances of the state were thwarted by both local officials and elites.

Yuan Shikai (1859–1916): Military leader of the late Qing. He commanded the modernized Beiyang Army in northern China. In 1898, he supported the suppression of the reformers. In 1911, he negotiated the abdication of the emperor and secured the presidency of the new Republic for himself. After an abortive attempt to assume the throne in 1916, he fled Beijing and died shortly thereafter.

Zeng Guofan (1811–1872): Military leader and provincial-level official who led the Hunan army against the Taipings in the 1860s. He played a leading role in the early Self-Strengthening Movement.

Zhang Juzheng (d. 1582): Chief grand secretary for the young Wanli emperor, he supervised much of the Single Whip tax reforms. His attempt to carry out an empire-wide survey of landholdings to revise the tax registers was resisted by local literati elites.

Zhang Xueliang (1898–2001): Warlord in northwestern China who placed Chiang Kaishek under house arrest in December 1936 to coerce him into forming a new alliance with the Communists to resist Japanese aggression. After the negotiations concluded and Chiang was released, he placed Zhang under arrest; Zhang was held by the Nationalists until 1996.

Zhu Di (1360–1424): Third emperor of the Ming dynasty. Fourth son of Zhu Yuanzhang, Zhu Di resented the naming of his nephew as emperor in 1398 and soon rebelled. He captured Nanjing in 1402 and took the throne for himself.

Zhu Xi (1130–1200): Philosopher who brought together ideas about natural patterns and principles and the nature of moral values to synthesize the school of *Daoxue*, the "Learning of the Way." His interpretations of the Confucian classics became the standard for the imperial examination system from the mid-13th century on.

Zhu Yuanzhang (1328–1398): Founding emperor of the Ming dynasty. He rose from being an impoverished orphan to become leader of the Red Turbans rebel movement at the end of the Yuan. In 1368, he defeated the last Mongol forces and established his new regime. His paranoia about the literati led him to launch repeated purges of his officials, claiming tens of thousands of victims.

Zhuangzi (late 4th–early 3rd centuries B.C.E.): Philosopher who developed and interpreted the teachings of Laozi. He emphasized the relativity to knowledge and the ideas of uselessness and emptiness.

Zhuge Liang (181–234): General known for his clever stratagems during the Three Kingdoms period. He was an advisor to Liu Bei, ruler of the Shu Han kingdom in modern Sichuan.

Bibliography

Abu-Lughod, Janet L. *Before European Hegemony*. Oxford: Oxford University Press, 1989. An overview of the Eurasian economic world before the age of Western exploration and expansion.

Bergere, Marie-Claire. *Sun Yat-sen*. Berkeley: University of California Press, 2001. The definitive biography of the Nationalist leader.

Bianco, Lucien. *Origins of the Chinese Revolution, 1915–1949*. Stanford: Stanford University Press, 1967. Bianco untangles the complex interaction of elite and mass politics from the warlord era through the establishment of the People's Republic in 1949, tracing the ways in which the Chinese Communist Party addressed the felt needs of both peasants and intellectuals and provided leadership in the struggle to resist Japan and oppose Western domination.

Bol, Peter K. *This Culture of Ours*. Stanford: Stanford University Press, 1992. Traces the transformation of the *shi* elite from the Tang through the early Song and the ways in which this development led to a reconfiguration of Chinese intellectual culture.

Brook, Timothy. *The Confusions of Pleasure*. Berkeley: University of California Press, 1998. An economic and cultural history of the Ming dynasty, focusing on the tensions and social changes engendered by growth and prosperity through the 15th and 16th centuries.

Chaffee, John W. *The Thorny Gates of Learning in Sung China*. Albany: State University of New York Press, 1995. In this work, Chaffee develops his analysis of the ways in which the imperial examination system became the central focus of elite culture from the Song dynasty through later imperial history.

Chang, Kwang-chih. *The Archaeology of Ancient China*. New Haven: Yale University Press, 1977. Surveys the development of Chinese civilization from Paleolithic times through the unification of China under the Qin dynasty in 221 B.C.E.

Chen, Jo-shui. *Liu Tsung-yuan and Intellectual Change in T'ang China, 773–819*. Cambridge, UK: Cambridge University Press, 1992. Traces the life and intellectual career of one of the major proponents of *guwen* literary thought and the Confucian revival in the later Tang dynasty.

Chow, Tse-tsung. *The May Fourth Movement*. Stanford: Stanford University Press, 1960. A comprehensive account of the events of May 4, 1919, and the popular cultural and political movement that grew from them.

Cohen, Paul A., and John Schrecker. *Reform in Nineteenth Century China*. Cambridge, MA: Harvard University Press, 1976. A collection of essays on many dimensions of reform, including social, economic, and cultural efforts, as well as the mainstream of political activity.

Crossley, Pamela Kyle. *A Translucent Mirror*. Berkeley: University of California Press, 1999. A study of the creation of the Manchus by Nurhaci and their subsequent rise to imperial power in China, with special attention to the ideology of Manchu rule over the empire.

Dardess, John. *A Ming Society*. Berkeley: University of California Press, 1996. A study of the local history of one county in Jiangxi province that provides a window on the complex social history of China from the 14th to the 17th centuries.

deBary, William Theodore, and Irene Bloom, eds. *Sources of Chinese Tradition*, vol. 1. New York: Columbia University Press, 1999. A massive compendium of original source material in translation. This volume provides direct access to the ideas and arguments that shaped China's cultural development, from its origins through the 16th century.

Dien, Albert, ed. *State and Society in Early Medieval China*. Stanford: Stanford University Press, 1990. A collection of essays on the complex and little studied period from the end of the Han through the Sui reunification, focusing on the social and cultural transformations that took place over these three and a half centuries.

Dirlik, Arif. *Anarchism in the Chinese Revolution*. Berkeley: University of California Press, 1991. Traces the role of anarchist thought and the actions of early Chinese anarchists in the development of revolutionary movements in China in the early 20th century.

Dreyer, Edward L. *Early Ming China*. Stanford: Stanford University Press, 1982. A political history of the establishment of the Ming dynasty and the reigns of the first five emperors, emphasizing the continuities with Mongol rule and the ways in which the early Ming differed from the dynasty's later, more mature phase.

Endicott-West, Elizabeth. *Mongolian Rule in China*. Cambridge, MA: Harvard University Press, 1989. An examination of the workings of local administration under the Mongols, including the use of non-Chinese officials to staff many positions and limit the influence of the literati elite.

Esherick, Joseph W. *Reform and Revolution in China*. Berkeley: University of California Press, 1976. A study of the 1911 revolution that brought down the Qing dynasty, focusing on the events in Hunan and Hubei provinces, which were central to the outbreak and spread of radical activities.

———. *The Origins of the Boxer Uprising*. Berkeley: University of California Press, 1987. Traces the background of the Boxer movement in rural Shandong province, with special emphasis on the social history of martial arts and secret societies.

Fingarette, Herbert. *Confucius: The Secular as Sacred*. New York: Harper & Row, 1972. A philosophical reflection on the Confucian concept of the nature of ritual and its role in social relationships. Fingarette is not a China scholar but approaches Confucius in a cross-cultural encounter that he believes can yield useful insights for the modern West.

Fitzgerald, John. *Awakening China*. Stanford: Stanford University Press, 1996. An analysis of the political and cultural programs of the Nationalist Party in the 1930s and their impact on society and government in a time of great change and upheaval.

Fong, Wen, ed. *Beyond Representation*. New Haven: Yale University Press, 1992. An art history of the transformation of painting during the Song dynasty. Painting moved away from the direct representation of observed things and began to portray the inner patterns, the *li*, of Neo-Confucian thinking.

Gardner, Daniel K. *Chu Hsi and the Ta-hsueh*. Cambridge, MA: Harvard University Press, 1986. A discussion of Zhu Xi's revision of the canon of Confucian texts in the 12th century. Gardner uses Zhu Xi's textual reorganization to explore his ideas on learning and the proper ordering of society, as well as his views on the origins of moral values.

Gernet, Jacques. *Buddhism in Chinese Society*. New York: Columbia University Press, 1995. Despite the title, this is essentially an economic history of Buddhism in the Tang dynasty. The rise of monasteries as landholders became a major issue for imperial finances and was an important element in the Confucian critique of Buddhism in the 8th and 9th centuries.

Gilley, Bruce. *Tiger on the Brink*. Berkeley: University of California Press, 1998. A biography of Jiang Zemin, China's prime minister after 1989. Gilley explores Jiang's career as a prototype of the new technocratic elite emerging as the rulers of China in the 21st century.

Goodman, Howard. *Ts'ao P'i Transcendent*. Seattle: Scripta Serica, 1998. A detailed study of the process of the founding of the Three Kingdom-era state of Wei in the early 220s. Goodman presents the political culture of this period through extensive study of the official rhetoric and actions of political and military leaders.

Hammond, Kenneth J., ed. *The Human Tradition in Premodern China*. Wilmington, DE: Scholarly Resources, 2002. A collection of biographical essays on individuals from throughout Chinese history, ranging from a Shang royal consort to a Ming merchant, a legalist prime minister of the Qin to a Tang writer.

Hansen, Valerie. *Changing Gods in Medieval China, 1127–1276*. Princeton: Princeton University Press, 1990. Presents the effects of commercialization on the social and cultural history of the Southern Song dynasty through a study of the spread of religious cults by itinerant merchants.

Hartman, Charles. *Han Yu and the T'ang Search for Unity*. Princeton: Princeton University Press, 1986. A biography and literary history of Han Yu and the *guwen* movement, with extensive translations of Han Yu's writings. Provides both an insightful treatment of one Chinese intellectual and an overview of one of the most creative periods in Chinese history.

Hinton, William. *Fanshen: A Documentary of Revolution in a Chinese Village*. Berkeley: University of California Press, 1966. A fascinating firsthand account of the process of land reform and rural revolution in a single village in northwest China in the late 1940s.

Hsu, Cho-yun, and Katheryn M. Linduff. *Western Chou Civilization*. New Haven: Yale University Press, 1988. An in-depth study of the archaeology and history of the Zhou dynasty from its founding around 1045 B.C.E. to the middle of the 8th century B.C.E.

Huang, Ray. *1587: A Year of No Significance*. New Haven: Yale University Press, 1981. Using a single year in the late Ming, Huang presents a detailed analysis of the workings of the imperial state and the tensions and challenges faced by officials in making and carrying out government policies.

Hymes, Robert P., and Conrad Schirokauer, eds. *Ordering the World*. Berkeley: University of California Press, 1993. An anthology of essays on statecraft theory and practice in the Song dynasty, emphasizing the ways in which changes in Confucian thought were reflected in state policies.

Jing, Jun. *The Temple of Memories*. Stanford: Stanford University Press, 1996. A study of the revival of the cult of Confucius in a village in northwest China in the 1990s, where collateral descendants of the sage rebuilt a temple destroyed during the Cultural Revolution.

Johnson, Chalmers. *Peasant Nationalism and Communist Power*. Stanford: Stanford University Press, 1962. The classic analysis of how the Chinese Communist Party achieved widespread support among the peasants of northern China by leading the guerilla resistance to Japanese invasion.

Keightley, David N. *The Ancestral Landscape*. Berkeley: Institute of East Asian Studies, 2000. Keightley is, perhaps, the leading expert on the oracle bone inscriptions of the Shang period, and in this book, he draws on a lifetime of study to present a synthetic portrait of Shang political culture.

Kuhn, Philip A. *Soulstealers: The Chinese Sorcery Scare of 1768*. Cambridge, MA: Harvard University Press, 1990. A case study of how the Qing dynasty dealt with popular unrest and insecurity during the reign of the Qianlong emperor. Kuhn presents the internal workings of the Qing bureaucracy clearly and situates them in the context of relations between the literate elite and broader mass society.

Lee, Hong Yong. *The Politics of the Chinese Cultural Revolution*. Berkeley: University of California Press, 1978. A local history of the Cultural Revolution in Guangdong province in southern China, showing how the national political conflicts that sparked the movement intertwined with local realities.

Levathes, Louise. *When China Ruled the Seas*. New York: Simon & Schuster, 1994. A popular account of the voyages led by the eunuch Zheng He between 1405 and 1435, which took Chinese fleets throughout Southeast Asia, the Indian Ocean, and the east coast of Africa.

Lewis, Mark Edward. *Sanctioned Violence in Early China*. Albany: State University of New York Press, 1990. Examines how forms of violence were incorporated into Chinese social and political life from the origins of Chinese states through the Han dynasty, showing how China was transformed from a network of "city states" into a unified territorial empire.

Liu, Xinru. *Ancient India and Ancient China*. Delhi: Oxford University Press, 1988. By exploring the trade and religious exchanges between these two ancient civilizations, Liu offers a basis for understanding the migration of Buddhism into China and for China's ongoing interaction with the Indian realm.

Loewe, Michael, and Edward L. Shaughnessy, eds. *The Cambridge History of Ancient China*. Cambridge, UK: Cambridge University Press, 1999. This monumental volume brings together definitive essays on the archaeology and history of China from the origins of civilization through the Qin unification in 221 B.C.E.

MacFarquhar, Roderick, ed. *The Politics of China: The Eras of Mao and Deng*. Cambridge, UK: Cambridge University Press, 1997. An anthology of essays on the political history of China from 1949 through the early 1990s. Particular attention is given to the role of elite politics.

McNair, Amy. *The Upright Brush*. Honolulu: University of Hawai'i Press, 1998. A study of the development of calligraphy as a major literati art form in the Song dynasty and of how models from the Tang were used to establish schools of theory and practice.

Meisner, Maurice. *Mao's China and After*. New York: The Free Press, 1999. A comprehensive history of China from the late 1940s through the reforms of the 1980s and 1990s. Meisner situates elite political conflict in the broader context of China's social and economic development.

Miyazaki, Ichisada. *China's Examination Hell*. New Haven: Yale University Press, 1981. A brief but thorough presentation of the imperial civil service examination system as it operated during the last 1,000 years of dynastic history.

Mote, Frederick W. *Intellectual Foundations of China*. New York: McGraw-Hill, 1989. A concise discussion of the main schools of thought emerging in Warring States China and the main thinkers associated with each of them.

Munro, Donald J. *Images of Human Nature*. Princeton: Princeton University Press, 1988. A biography of Zhu Xi that traces the development of key ideas in the formation of his Neo-Confucian thought, emphasizing the tension between family life and the state, which remains an important dimension of China's contemporary political order.

Naquin, Susan, and Evelyn S. Rawski. *Chinese Society in the Eighteenth Century*. New Haven: Yale University Press, 1987. A social and economic portrait of China during an age of great achievements and impending changes and challenges.

Pearce, Scott, Audrey Shapiro, and Patricia Ebrey, eds. *Culture and Power in the Reconstitution of the Chinese Realm, 200–600*. Cambridge, MA: Harvard University Press, 2001. A collection of essays exploring the complex social and economic history of the long period of disunity following the fall of the Han and encompassing the migration of Inner Asian peoples into northern China.

Perry, Elizabeth J. *Rebels and Revolutionaries in North China, 1845–1945*. Stanford: Stanford University Press, 1980. A local history of poverty and social unrest in northern Anhui and western Shandong provinces, which were the homelands of some of the main rebel movements of the later Qing dynasty, including the Boxer movement of the 1890s.

Polachek, James. *The Inner Opium War*. Cambridge, MA: Harvard University Press, 1992. A major study of the internal political debates and conflicts over how to deal with the opium problem among Chinese officials in the 1830s and 1840s. Reveals a great deal about the workings of the late imperial political system.

Ratchnevsky, Paul. *Genghis Khan: His Life and Legacy*. Oxford: Blackwell Publishers, 1992. A biography of Temujin, the founder and first great leader of the Mongols during their age of expansion and conquest in the early 13th century.

Roberts, Moss, trans. *Three Kingdoms: A Historical Novel*. Berkeley: University of California Press, 1992. One of the great classical Chinese novels, *Three Kingdoms* is filled with the romance and adventure of this period of military glory and political frustration.

Rossabi, Morris, ed. *China among Equals*. Berkeley: University of California Press, 1983. A collection of essays on the interstate system of China and its neighbors from the 10th through the 14th centuries, when non-Chinese peoples ruled part, and sometimes all, of the territory usually considered China.

———. *Khubilai Khan*. Berkeley: University of California Press, 1988. A biography of the Mongol grandson of Chinggis Khan, who became the first alien ruler over all of China with the final conquest of the Southern Song in 1279. Khubilai was emperor of the Yuan dynasty until his death in 1296 and was host to Marco Polo during his years in China.

Salisbury, Harrison. *The Long March*. New York: Harper & Row, 1985. In the early 1980s, Salisbury set out to retrace the course of the epic journey of the Chinese Communists in 1934–1935. This book is the result of that effort and includes interviews with survivors and Salisbury's own reflections on the endurance and heroism of the Long Marchers.

Saunders, J. J. *The History of the Mongol Conquests*. London: Routledge & Kegan Paul, 1971. An overview of the military campaigns that took the Mongols from the obscurity of the Inner Asian grasslands to near total domination of the Eurasian landmass in the course of the 13th century.

Schwartz, Benjamin. *In Search of Wealth and Power*. Cambridge, MA: Harvard University Press, 1964. A study of the life and thought of Yan Fu, one of the most important figures in the intellectual reform of China in the late 19th and early 20th centuries.

———. *The World of Thought in Ancient China*. Cambridge, MA: Harvard University Press, 1985. A history and analysis of the main streams of thought in China down to the Han dynasty. Schwartz places Confucius at the heart of this story and builds his portrait of the many schools and thinkers around this focal point.

Sima, Qian. *The Records of the Grand Historian: Qin Dynasty*. New York: Columbia University Press, 1993. Sima Qian was the first great historian of ancient China. This is a translation of parts of his history of the rise and rule of the Qin dynasty, including his biography of the first Qin emperor.

Snow, Edgar. *Red Star over China*. New York: Grove Press, 1968. Snow was an American journalist who traveled to the Communist base area in northwest China and was able to interview many of the Communist leaders, including Mao Zedong, as well as survivors of the Long March. This book, originally published in 1938, includes the first account in the West of Mao and his ideas.

Spence, Jonathan. *God's Chinese Son*. New York: W.W. Norton & Co., 1996. A biography of Hong Xiuquan and a history of the Taiping Heavenly Kingdom, which he founded and led in the most serious challenge to Qing power since the 17th century.

―――. *K'ang-hsi, Emperor of China*. New York: Alfred A. Knopf, 1974. Based on the emperor's own writings, Spence creates a human-scale portrait of one of the greatest rulers in China's history. Kangxi is shown not only as a political leader but as a family man, with concerns about his children and his own health alongside the major administrative issues on his mind.

―――. *Mao Zedong*. New York: Viking Books, 1999. A short, highly readable account of the life and times of China's great modern revolutionary leader. Spence presents a careful, balanced story of the man without whom, the Chinese say, there would be no New China.

Tillman, Hoyt Cleveland, and Stephen H. West, eds. *China under Jurchen Rule*. Albany: State University of New York Press, 1995. An anthology of writings about the Jin dynasty, when the Jurchen people controlled northern China, and how Chinese scholars found roles both in government and in carrying on the cultural life of the literati under alien rule.

Twitchett, Denis, and Michael Loewe, eds. *The Cambridge History of China*, Volume 1: *The Ch'in and Han Empires*. Cambridge, UK: Cambridge University Press, 1986. The first volume in the authoritative 14-volume series. Includes essays on the political, military, legal, economic, and social history of the formative centuries of China's classic imperial order.

Wakeman, Frederick. *Strangers at the Gate*. Berkeley: University of California Press, 1966. A study of the social impact of the Opium War in Guangdong province, showing how ordinary Chinese responded to the defeat of the Qing and the intrusion of Western power into their local environment.

―――. *The Great Enterprise*. Berkeley: University of California Press, 1985. A massive two-volume study of the rise of the Manchus and their conquest and consolidation of power in the 17th century. The most thorough account of power, politics, and military affairs available.

Wang, Aihe. *Cosmology and Political Culture in Early China.* Cambridge, UK: Cambridge University Press, 2000. Explores the intricate links between ideas about the underlying order of the natural world and the human realm. Social order was seen as part of the natural world, and natural phenomena could be read as omens and portents with implications for government.

Watson, Burton, trans. *Han Fei Tzu: Basic Writings.* New York: Columbia University Press, 1964. Presents the fundamental ideas of the philosopher most associated with Legalism and the rise of the Qin dynasty.

————, trans. *Mo Tzu: Basic Writings.* New York: Columbia University Press, 1963. Selections from the writings of one of the most creative thinkers of the Warring States period, who emphasized doctrines of universal love and the rejection of aggressive warfare in an age of chronic conflict.

Whitfield, Susan. *Life along the Silk Road.* Berkeley: University of California Press, 1999. Describes the lives of a variety of people, from merchants to monks, in the oasis towns along the Silk Road, the vital overland trade link between China and India, Persia and the Mediterranean.

Wriggins, Sally Hovey. *Xuanzang: A Buddhist Pilgrim on the Silk Road.* Boulder, CO: Westview Press, 1996. The story of the Tang dynasty Buddhist pilgrim who walked from China to India and back, bringing treasures of Buddhist scriptures with him that transformed the understanding of Buddhism in China.

Wright, Arthur F. *Buddhism in Chinese History.* Stanford: Stanford University Press, 1959. A concise overview of the basic teachings of Buddhism and how it came to China and developed in interaction with Chinese civilization.

————. *The Sui Dynasty.* New York: Alfred A. Knopf, 1978. The history of the reunification of China by Yang Jian in the late 6th century and the flourishing and collapse of the Sui dynasty he founded and passed on to his son, Yang Guang.

Wright, Arthur F., and Denis Twitchett, eds. *Perspectives on the T'ang.* New Haven: Yale University Press, 1973. Essays on the social and political history of the Tang, as well as Tang thought and religion and the great age of Chinese poetry.

Xiong, Victor Cunrui. *Sui-Tang Chang'an.* Ann Arbor: University of Michigan, Center for Chinese Studies, 2000. A history of the great urban center of Chang'an, capital of the Sui and Tang dynasties and the largest city in the world. As the economic center of the Tang Empire, Chang'an was host to traders and travelers from across the Eurasian continent.

Yang, Ye. *Vignettes from the Late Ming*. Seattle: University of Washington Press, 1999. An anthology of translations of short writings from the Ming dynasty. These occasional pieces provide unique insights into the intellectual concerns and social alienation of the literati in a time of deepening crisis for the dynastic state.

Yoshinobu, Shiba. *Commerce and Society in Sung China*. Ann Arbor: University of Michigan, Center for Chinese Studies, 1992. An important study by a Japanese scholar of the dynamics of growth that reshaped China from the 11th through the early 13th centuries and that drove the transformation of much of the East Asian economic order, as well.

Notes

Notes